LONDON IN THE COUNTRY

BY THE SAME AUTHOR

The Black Treasures of Scotland Yard

GUY R. WILLIAMS

London in the Country

THE GROWTH OF SUBURBIA

HAMISH HAMILTON
LONDON

First published in Great Britain 1975
by Hamish Hamilton Ltd.
90 Great Russell Street London WC1

SBN 241 89193 0

Printed in Great Britain by
Western Printing Services Ltd., Bristol

CONTENTS

ILLUSTRATIONS

Between pages 54 *and* 55

Between pages 150 *and* 151

Illustrations 1, 8a and 8b are reproduced by kind permission of London Transport; 2a and 2b by kind permission of the London Borough of Harrow Library Service; 3a by kind permission of the London Borough of Barnet Library Services; 3b by kind permission of Flight International; 4a by kind permission of the Hampstead Garden Suburb Institute; 4b by kind permission of the London Borough of Enfield Public Libraries; 5a by kind permission of the London Borough of Waltham Forest, Museum of Local History; 5b by kind permission of the London Borough of Newham Library Service; 6a and 7b by kind permission of Greenwich Local History Library; 6b by kind permission of the Trustee of the Martin Collection, London Borough of Greenwich Local History Library; 7a, 9a, 9b, 9c, 15a and 15b by kind permission of the National Portrait Gallery, London; 10a and 10b by kind permission of Merton Public Libraries; 11a, 11b, 12a, 12b and 13 by kind permission of the London Borough of Richmond upon Thames; 14a, 14b, 16a and 16b by kind permission of the London Borough of Hounslow Library Services: Chiswick Library.

ACKNOWLEDGMENTS

In compiling this book, I have been helped enormously by the Chief Information Officer, the Chief Librarian, or the Local History Librarian of each of the following London boroughs—Barking, Barnet, Bexley, Brent, Bromley, Camden, Croydon, Ealing, Enfield, Greenwich, Hackney, Haringey, Harrow, Havering, Hillingdon, Hounslow, Kingston upon Thames, Lambeth, Lewisham, Merton, Newham, Redbridge, Richmond upon Thames, Southwark, Sutton, Tower Hamlets, Waltham Forest and Wandsworth. In some boroughs I have been helped by two of those official persons. In a few, I have been helped by all three. And, their assistants have been unfailingly co-operative.

Some of these kind people have asked me not to mention them, in my acknowledgments, by name. That being so, it would seem invidious to name the others. All, wanting to be named or not wanting to be named, have been unstintingly generous and have given me so much of their time and attention that I can only say 'Thank you very much' and hope that I have not inadvertently misinterpreted any of the information they have so enthusiastically tried to pass on to me.

I am also most grateful to Raymond Alwin-Hill, for help with research; to Miss Barbara Harris, for checking and typing my manuscript so carefully; and to Miss Helen Thomson, for finding the interesting illustrations.

CHAPTER ONE

The Suburbs of London

'WHAT a Monster must London be, extending from the farther end of Chelsea, West, to Deptford-Bridge, East', wrote Daniel Defoe. At that time—the end of the seventeenth century—London was little more than one hundredth its present size, the World's End pub at Chelsea being then, as now, less than seven miles, as the crow flies, from the old shipbuilding yards below the Pool. Defoe would have been amazed if he had foreseen what a veritable Monster London would ultimately become, with the capital of England extending, today, from Uxbridge in the west to Great Warley and North Ockenden in the east, a distance of approximately thirty-five miles. And, the metropolitan area is still expanding.

By the middle of the eighteenth century, a few of the settlements that were separated from the capital by less than a dozen miles of open country, having springs which produced water with real or assumed medicinal qualities, had become known as spas or watering places. None of them had quite as much prestige as Bath or Epsom, which acted like magnets to the fashionable world, but Hampstead, Islington and Muswell Hill to the north of the Thames, and Camberwell, Dulwich, Richmond, Streatham and Sydenham to the south of the river definitely grew in size and importance because they could offer therapeutic benefits, however dubious, in an age when sickness and pain were regarded as normal ingredients of the almost intolerable human condition.

At the close of the eighteenth century, most of the small settlements that were scattered in a roughly drawn ring round the capital still consisted of a few houses only, grouped in a more or less haphazard fashion round a village green, which would be watered by a pond or well and given an individual Christian identity by the presence of a church. The district we now call 'Hampstead' had no fewer than six such separate clusters of dwellings, identifiable to this day as New End, North End, South End, West End, Church

End and Fortune Green. Hornsey, a little to the east, had its Crouch End, Fortis Green and Stroud Green. All these hamlets have been completely submerged now in suburban sprawl, but most of their melodious names—ending, almost invariably, with the words 'End' or 'Green'—have managed, miraculously, to survive into the last quarter of the twentieth century and can still charm and delight us when we encounter them unexpectedly on local signposts or in a list of places on the front, back or sides of an omnibus.

London did not start to spread its boundaries outwards at any great speed until Defoe had been dead for over a hundred years. Then, the sprawl began in earnest—impelled, to a certain extent, by a change in popular thinking that may not have been entirely unconnected with the revolution that had taken place in France, or with the sentiments expressed so forcibly in England during the Gordon riots.

For several centuries, the powerful and the rich had known the advantages of having a place in the country as well as a place in the town. The royal families had had palaces at Eltham, Greenwich, Hampton, Kew, Nonsuch, Shene and Windsor to which they could escape from the bugs and the fevers and the smells of the cities of London and Westminster. The Dukes of Devonshire and Northumberland had had similar pastoral retreats at Chiswick and Sion. Early in the nineteenth century, the possibility that they might be able to live at some distance from their normal places of work began to dawn on other members of the community whose hereditary circumstances were not so rare and exalted.

The idea had an immediate appeal to those who were prepared to walk quite long distances to and from their homes. Mr. Wemmick, the lawyer's clerk in Charles Dickens' *Great Expectations*, was an archetypal foot-commuter. His little cottage in Walworth, done up like a castle with crenellations, a tiny moat, a drawbridge, and a cannon that could be fired at nine o'clock every night, Greenwich time, allowed Mr. Wemmick to escape in fantasy as well as in topographical fact from the grim realities of Mr. Jaggers' office in which Mr. Wemmick worked during the day, and which was hard by the squalid precincts of the prison at Newgate. Like many more recent dwellers in London's suburbs, Mr. Wemmick insisted on a strict division being kept between the thoughts proper to his place of work, and those suitable to the miniature citadel he shared with his father, the Ancient, and at which he was visited by the attractive but decorous Miss Skiffins. ('Walworth is one place, and this office is another . . . They must not be confounded together. My Walworth sentiments must be taken at Walworth: none but my official sentiments can be taken in this office'.) Walworth, today, is well supplied with men and women who have Mr. Wemmick's capacity for opening and closing the appropriate sections of their minds, according to their whereabouts.

In 1829, the way of the commuter was made just a little easier when George Shillibeer started London's first omnibus service with a small fleet of horse-drawn carriages that ran between Paddington Green and the Bank of England. Within four years, six hundred of these slow and dreadfully uncomfortable conveyances were operating in London, moving thousands of passengers each morning from the West End to the City and back again at the end of the day. By 1834, the competition among horse omnibus proprietors had become so fierce that Shillibeer, the doyen of them all, was driven out of business. He lived to see the wide open spaces around Kilburn and Kensal Green covered with houses as a result of his enterprise.

The years 1827 to 1836 saw London's first successful experiments with mechanical road transport. The inventor of the 'steam road coach'—an engineer named Walter Hancock, who had premises in the High Street at Stratford—spent those years developing a series of steam-driven vehicles which he called, successively, the *Infant*, the *Era*, the *Enterprise*, the *Autopsy* (without, apparently, thought of any coroner's inquest that might result from his activities), and, finally, the *Automaton*, his most ambitious venture, which could move at twenty miles per hour with its maximum load of twenty-two passengers. Hancock's conveyances ran for varying periods on routes that led from Stratford to London, and from the City to the rapidly developing areas around Paddington. With the *Automaton*, Hancock decided to extend the range of his business. As the *Morning Herald* reported, on 25 October, 1836:

> . . . With a view to further testing the practicability of steam conveyance on common roads, Mr. Walter Hancock, accompanied by a party of gentlemen interested in mechanical inventions, started on Friday morning in his steam carriage, the

'Automaton', from his station in the City Road to Epping. This line of road was selected on account of its being, for the distance, the most hilly and uneven out of the Metropolis, as well as satisfying his friends that, even with this disadvantage, from the improvements which he had introduced, the carriage would perform at least ten miles per hour, and the result proved that he had underestimated its power. On arriving at Woodford, Mr. Hancock stopped the carriage in front of the house of Mr. Rounding, the sign of the 'Horse and Groom', who kindly procured a fresh supply of water. After remaining for nearly a quarter of an hour, Mr. Hancock again started at a rapid pace, and having ascended Buckhurst Hill at the rate of at least 7½ m.p.h., entered Epping among the loud cheers of some thousands who were collected in the town, it being market day . . .

When the first steam-powered passenger-carrying railways started to operate in the London area, the capital covered less than one hundred square miles and its population was under two million souls.

The first sod for the London and Birmingham Railway was cut at Chalk Farm on the first day of June 1834. In 1837, parts of that historic line were declared open. The London and Southampton Railway (called, later, the 'South-Western') was finished by 1840, and the Great Western, joining Paddington to Bristol, was completed in the following year. The coming of the steam train was to change the outer shape of London dramatically, but it did not have a great immediate effect, since hardly any of the operating companies were interested, at first, in purely local traffic. Then, gradually, as a network of suburban lines was built up, the possibilities offered by the new form of transport became apparent to an increasing number of people, and London started, almost literally, to explode.

Predictably, it was the well-to-do who moved out of the centre of London first, building their solid, comfortable Victorian mansions within easy walking distance of the railway stations of their choice. Some of these houses can still be seen, these 'Portman Villas' and 'Beaufort Lodges', within a short stone's throw of such stations as Mortlake and Penge, though their original gardens will probably have been sadly reduced.

Then, after 1860, thousands of clerks and shopkeepers and small salary-earners began to seek villas 'a little way out of town'. Their efforts were largely self-defeating, though. Soon, in the urban Music Halls, unkind singers were deriding these would-be country dwellers:

Oh, it really is a werry pretty garden
  And Chingford to Eastwood could be seen
Wiv a ladder and some glasses
You could see to 'Ackney Marshes
  If it wasn't for the 'ouses in between.

A little later, again, than that, the pressures of London's ever-increasing population, the freeing of the highways from tolls, the development of tram services and the introduction of cheap 'workmen's fares' on the railways led to the rapid growth of predominantly working-class suburbs such as Tottenham. London's most significant expansion of all was seen in the years between the First and Second World Wars, when the metropolitan built-up area approximately doubled. The London County Council alone erected nearly 100,000 dwellings during this period—half of them, on land outside the County of London.

So, the area to be covered by this book is extensive, and it is also extremely varied. Any attempt to be selective in such a wide field will inevitably lay an author open to charges of being arbitrary, of failing to deal with places or subjects that the reader considers to be of the utmost importance. But where—to deal only with the problem of geographical limitation—as one moves further and further from Charing Cross, the point from which such measurements have traditionally been taken, do London's suburbs start? And where, at the outer periphery, may they be fairly said to end?

About this question, the definition of the evocative noun 'suburb' given by the *New English Dictionary*—'an outlying part of a city or a town'—is not particularly helpful, for it does not specify how far any part of a metropolitan area has to be situated from the centre before it can be fairly said to 'lie out'. More guidance may come, possibly, from the same dictionary's definition of the adjective 'suburban'—of purely local interest. With that, we are on safer ground. There was once, around London, as we have seen, a roughly circular ring of countrified villages and hamlets whose worthy inhabitants interested themselves principally in purely local affairs. This book, then, shall be a survey of the most important of these quiet and homely places. Suburbs, they may have become, but each, with its long history, contains something that may be of interest to visitors, as well as to those who have spent all their lives within sight and sound of the old parish pump.

CHAPTER TWO

Harrow—with Wealdstone, Pinner, Hatch End and Stanmore

HARROW is principally famous for three things—its hill, its church, and, above all, its school.

Harrow Hill rises, abrupt and isolated, to a height of some two hundred feet above the surrounding plain. Geologists tell us that it is a mass of London clay capped with sand—an 'outlier', in fact, of the far more extensive Bagshot sands. With the spire of the church crowning and giving dignity and distinction to its summit, Harrow Hill is a conspicuous and pleasing feature of the landscape for many miles, from every side. (When King Charles II heard some eminent theologians discussing 'the only visible church', he thought they were referring to Harrow.)

The town of Harrow that occupies the crest of the hill and clothes some of its slopes has a relatively ancient history. Long before the Norman Conquest, it is known, the manor of Harrow belonged to the Archbishops of Canterbury. It passed out of their possession in 1543 when Archbishop Cranmer gave it to King Henry VIII in exchange for other lands. Henry kept the manor for three years only, before he handed it on to Lord North.

Twenty years before the manor of Harrow ceased to be ecclesiastical property, the place attracted much public attention when some wise persons predicted that on the first day of February 1524 there would be a flood even greater than the one that Noah had survived. The waters of the Thames would rise to such tremendous heights, they asserted, that ten thousand London houses would be washed away. (Prognostications of the same kind are still being made today.) Their prophecy was widely believed, and it is said that by the middle of that January twenty thousand people had deserted the 'doomed' city.

Among the refugees was William Bolton, the prior of St. Bartholomew's, who may well have designed the great Chapel at

Westminster for King Henry VII. (He is referred to, in the king's will, as 'Maister-of-the-Works'.) Bolton, it was reported, took all the members of his household and the officers and brethren of the priory for safety out of London and up to Harrow, where he built 'a kind of fortress' to accommodate them, stocking it with sufficient food for two months' isolation and providing, too, boats and rowers in case the floods should rise higher than the summit of The Hill. Bolton went to all this trouble—need it be said?—in vain. There was no flood. For a time, the 'prophets' were in danger of losing their lives. They escaped, eventually, by discovering, happily, that they had made a mistake of exactly a century in their calculations.

The school at Harrow was founded in 1571 by John Lyon, a well-to-do yeoman who lived at Preston, a hamlet in the vicinity of The Hill. It was a revival of an ancient church school which had been allowed to disappear after the Reformation.

As the numbers of its pupils increased, the school's original building—the 'School House', with its single class-room, called today the 'Fourth Form Room'—became insufficiently commodious, and other buildings had to be put up. With admirable foresight, the governors of the school acquired much of the choicest land in the district, and today the suburb of Harrow-on-the-Hill owes its thoroughly distinctive character—a character that every visitor recognises instantly and realises to be quite unique—to the presence of the school.

Besides the extensive blocks used for tuition and learning, there are in the town a number of masters' houses that are each sufficiently large to accommodate a few dozen boy boarders, and these houses are mostly built in a cheerful 'domestic gothic' style that seems entirely appropriate. Among them, there are a number of shops—small, but delightful—which have catered to the needs of the members of the school for many generations. It is hardly surprising that with such a civilised atmosphere to enjoy, a number of fairly affluent people have chosen to live in the immediate neighbourhood. Many of the large private dwellings constructed to accommodate them have been built in the same style—gently reminiscent of North Oxford—as the school houses, so the influence of the school can be seen to be unusually pervasive.

Until 1839, the boys of Harrow School were required to go regularly to the parish church of St. Mary's, where, on the flat tomb of John Peachey, young Byron used to lie lazily (in the words of one of the school songs)

> Hid from lesson and game away,
> Dreaming poetry all alone,
> Up-a-top of the Peachey stone

In that year, however, a chapel intended especially for the boys' use was built at the north end of the High Street to the designs of a Mr. C. R. Cockerell, R.A. Cockerell's chapel was a neat, red brick structure that was intended to consort happily with the buildings in its immediate vicinity. At first, the school's new place of worship was much admired, but when the craze for the revived Gothic style started to sweep through England the serene simplicity of Cockerell's scheme was severely criticised. Fifteen years only, then, after it was erected, Cockerell's chapel was demolished, so that an entirely new chapel could be erected on its foundations to the designs of the infinitely more fashionable architect Sir Gilbert Scott, R.A., who had already spoiled the exterior of the ancient parish church by facing it with flints. Scott's chapel—'an elegant and admirably finished stone building of the thirteenth-century French type', noted a contemporary writer—was 'evidently modelled on the Ste. Chapelle, Paris'.

Near Scott's exotic piece of mock-medievalism there stands, today, another neo-Gothic structure designed by the same prolific Victorian, and intended to harmonise with it, rather than with the rest of the school buildings. This is the Vaughan Library, erected in memory of Doctor Vaughan who became Headmaster of Harrow in 1844. At that time, the school was in very low water—there were barely seventy pupils, and they were virtually unmanageable. Within two years of his appointment, Doctor Vaughan had raised the number of pupils to over two hundred, and by his teachings and example had managed to instil new life into the studies and discipline of the place. The library, said a contemporary observer, 'is a little fanciful in parts, but very pretty'. A little fanciful, too, but also very pretty is the silver-headed wand of office carried today by the senior prefect required to be 'on duty' in the library. There are superb views to be had from the terrace gardens at the rear of the library—on clear days, it is possible to see from there as far as Nettlebed, in Oxfordshire, some forty miles to the west, and Windsor Castle is often visible.

With public roads and shopping streets passing by, or through, almost every part of the school's premises, not much privacy can be expected by the school's deserving patrons. But there are a few occasions in the Harrow calendar of which only the really privileged can expect to get a glimpse.

There are the social gatherings on Speech Day, for instance. This colourful gala is traditionally held on The Hill on the first Thursday in June. On the very green lawns beside or behind the school's boarding houses there are routs of well-dressed parents, each of whom qualifies for an invitation by having a son, or sons, resident at that time, during school term, in that house. The refreshment provided is much appreciated, even though large picnic lunches have been consumed by most of those present, only a short time before, in remote corners of the school's playing fields or in its more rustic farmland. ('Don't put the champagne down just *there*, dear. The school cows have been here before us.') Still, there have been the swimming races in 'Duckpuddle' or 'Ducker' —the school bathing place—to watch since then, and, for some, a slow climb back up The Hill, on foot.

Shortly after five, the guests move into Speech Room, or 'Speechers', the assembly hall of the school, built in 1874 and largely paid for from the Lyon Memorial Fund raised by Old Harrovians in 1871 to commemorate the tercentenary of the founding of the school.

In Speech Room, the members of the audience are tightly packed together—the ceremony, quite unlike anything that happens anywhere else in the world, is so popular that seats have actually to be balloted for. The members of the school's orchestra are seated on the stage. The choristers—healthy young men, contributed by every house in the school, and dressed in the traditional tail coats that Harrovians still wear on formal occasions—are ranged in ascending rows behind. Many of them have red or white carnations in their button-holes. The gay colours of the dresses and large hats worn by the female guests in the steeply raked tiers of hard chairs facing the choir make the rest of the interior of Speech Room look like a full-blown garden of flowers.

Almost to the very end of his life, Sir Winston Churchill—one of Harrow's least unsuccessful sons—returned regularly to his old school for 'Songs'. He would listen, always, with the greatest interest to the lines sung by a carefully selected new boy:

Five hundred faces, and all so strange!
Life in front of me—home behind.
I felt like a waif before the wind.
Tossed on an ocean of shock and change

He was deeply moved, as all present always are, by the poignancy of the ceremony's famous conclusion:

Forty years on, when far and asunder
Parted are those who are singing to-day,
When you look back, and forgetfully wonder
What you were like in your work and your play,
Then, it may be, there will often come o'er you,
Glimpses of notes like the catch of a song—
Visions of boyhood shall float then before you,
Echoes of dreamland shall bear them along

When the last verse is reached, and the Old Boys of the school—some of them, very, very old—having risen proudly in their places, sing:

Forty years on, growing older and older
Shorter in wind, as in memory long,
Feeble of foot, and rheumatic of shoulder,
What will it help you that once you were strong?

there are not many people in the audience who are visibly unmoved.

At the beginning of the nineteenth century, Harrow-on-the-Hill was surrounded by wide expanses of woodland and heath that were only very sparsely populated, if they were lived in at all. Then, in 1837, George Stephenson, who was building the London and Birmingham Railway, opened a station at Wealdstone, which was little more than a mile from Harrow church. Within a very few years, a settlement had developed around this station, and along the old road that led to, and past, the neighbouring hamlet of Green Hill. The houses and shops did not spread far at first, however, in spite of an offer made in 1858 by the directors of the railway company in an attempt to drum up trade. They would give a free first class season ticket to Euston for eleven years, they said, to the owner of every new house in the district that had an annual value of more than £50.

The real rush to build in this stretch of hitherto 'undiscovered' country did not start until 1880, when the Metropolitan Railway Company opened their station at Harrow-on-the-Hill. Between that year and the end of the century the population of Harrow nearly doubled, most of the new houses being built between the old and the new stations to accommodate the prosperous Londoners who wished understandably to have one foot in the country (where they could enjoy the blossom and the bees) and the other foot in the town (where they could earn the necessary 'spondulicks'.)

This praiseworthy objective was not to be realisable in the Harrow area for long, however, for during the present century speculative builders have covered the green fields around The Hill with small, cheap dwellings at such a rate that the district has become a gigantic dormitory town that is almost entirely lacking in character. The utter grimness of the monotonous roads in these ironically-named 'estates' is only relieved by the occasional views that can be obtained from them of the enchanting Hill, with its mellow buildings, and their surrounding greenery.

Pinner, a little to the west of Harrow, is also a large residential area, and has been since shortly after the railways reached it, but it still has at its centre the quaint old original village with many timbered houses. The fourteenth-century 'East End Farm Cottage' in Moss Lane is probably the oldest, and two inns, the 'Victory', in the High Street, and the 'Queen's Head', on the opposite side of the road, date from the seventeenth century. A fair held at Pinner on the Wednesday following Whitsun is an annual reminder of the charter granted by King Edward III in 1336 to John, Archbishop of Canterbury, which permitted the archbishop to hold each year two fairs and a market at 'his Manor of Pynnore'.

Buried in the cemetery in Paine's Lane, Pinner, is Horatia Nelson Ward, the daughter of Admiral Lord Nelson and Emma, Lady Hamilton. Nelson's letters to Lady Hamilton contain many affectionate references to the little child—his last message to Emma, written as the *Victory* sailed to its fatal engagement, ends with the words, 'I love you before any woman in this world, and next to you our dear Horatia'. After the death of Nelson, and during the sad decline of Emma into poverty and alcoholism, Horatia was principally cared for by her father's more orthodox and settled relatives. In the fulness of time, she married the Reverend Philip Ward, who was vicar of Tenterden, and bore him eight children. When the Reverend Ward retired, he and his wife moved to Pinner, where they lived in the house called Beaufort Villa at Woodridings. Their days at Pinner were marred by a tragic accident when one of their daughters was knocked down and killed by a horse that had bolted from the stable yard of the Queen's Head Tavern, previously mentioned.

Hatch End, a mile or two to the north-east of Pinner, was only a very small and isolated village at the beginning of this century. Since then it has developed rapidly as a suburb with a 'semi-countrified' air.

Harrow Weald—the broad and fairly level tract of land that extends northwards from Harrow Station as far as Stanmore—was once, as its name implies, a wild woodland. A little of Harrow Weald Common remains to this day: it runs up to the Watford road, and to the Hertfordshire border at Bushey Heath.

In this tract of ground beyond Harrow there have been, in the past few centuries, some exceptionally interesting buildings. The grandest of them all, without any doubt—Canons Park—was situated at Whitchurch, or Little Stanmore, which lies south and slightly to the east of Great Stanmore. Canons was the home of the ambitious profiteer James Brydges, First Duke of Chandos, who acquired a vast fortune by dubious means during the time that he was acting as Paymaster General to the Forces in the Duke of Marlborough's wars. When the wars were over, Brydges decided to spend a large part of his ill-gotten wealth on a house that would be worthy of his own importance, or what he judged to be his own importance. The mansion—called 'Canons' because it took the place of a manor that had belonged to the Augustinian canons of St. Bartholomew's—was built, fitted out and furnished by Brydges without regard to expense, even the locks and hinges on the doors being made of gold or silver.

Three years after the great man died, in 1744, his son found that he could not possibly afford to maintain such a magnificent place. Nobody else could afford to maintain it, either, it appeared, so the mansion had to be broken up and sold by lots, at auction, for as much as the various parts would fetch, which was not much. (The house is said to have cost, in all, around a quarter of a million pounds which, in today's terms, would be enough to put up several Centre Points. The auction produced just £11,000.) The great staircase was moved to the house that William Kent happened to be building in Mayfair for the Earl of Chesterfield. (It was moved again, when that house was demolished in 1934, to Harewood House in Yorkshire.) The iron gates went to the parish church at Hampstead. Other components were dispersed to far-flung parts of the United Kingdom, where they may not even be recognised, today, for what they have been.

The Canons Park estate was bought, then, by a cabinet maker named Hallett, who built on the site of the grand mansion a comparatively modest dwelling that has been used, since 1930, as a girls' school, namely the 'North London Collegiate'. Some parts of the Duke's lovely walled gardens have been acquired by the local authority and can now be freely enjoyed by members of the general public. (There is a particularly pleasant water garden there that has been dedicated to the memory of King George V.) The most compelling reminder of the Duke of Chandos' magnificence is the parish church of St. Lawrence, Whitchurch, which, in 1715, was largely rebuilt at His Grace's expense. Behind the altar, in this church, there is an organ on which Handel may well have played, during the time that he was on the Chandos' munificent payroll. (The great composer was employed at Canons for about two years, as the Duke's 'capell-meister'.) The memorial representation of the Duke himself, carved to life size, shows the great nobleman in a Roman toga and a full-bottomed wig. This is, sartorially, an improbable combination, but artistically it is remarkably effective.

The second of these out-of-the-ordinary buildings in the hinterland of Harrow is Bentley Priory. The original Priory—a religious establishment, as its name implies—was founded about the year 1170 by one Ranulf Glanvel, or Glanville. The old monastery has long since disappeared, its last remains having been pulled down in 1766 by the very rich army contractor James Duberly who happened to acquire the estate at that time. (He wanted to build for himself another residence, a little grander, and a little higher up Stanmore Hill, 'so that all could see his wealth and importance'.) Duberly's home was bought in 1790 by the Marquess of Abercorn and enlarged by him to the designs of Sir John Soane. Under Lord Abercorn's proud ownership—and, later, under the ownership of his son-in-law Lord Aberdeen, who succeeded to the property—the Priory became one of the most celebrated stately homes in the land.

When King William IV died in 1837, the Priory was let to the Dowager Queen Adelaide, and she lived there until she died in 1849. The house had an up-and-down career after that, being, at various times, the home of Sir James Kelk, the man responsible for building the Albert Memorial, a private residential hotel that was not particularly successful, a girls' school that did no better, and after 1924, an empty, echoing shell.

Then, after two years of disuse, the old mansion was purchased by the Air Ministry, with some forty acres of the surrounding ground. On 14 July, 1936, the men of Fighter Command moved into the Priory and established their headquarters there. So, it was from the Priory that Air Marshal Sir Hugh Dowding (later, Lord Dowding) supervised the Royal Air Force's efforts during the Battle of Britain in 1940. The house and grounds are still under Air Force control.

Much less difficult for the ordinary unauthorised person to view is Grim's Dyke House, the neo-Tudor mansion built for Frederick Goodall, the famous Victorian painter, from designs made by Norman Shaw who was also responsible, among many other notable buildings, for the old Scotland Yard citadel on the north bank of the Thames at Westminster. The house became in 1890 the home of Sir William Gilbert, the successful and wealthy playwright who had collaborated with Sir Arthur Sullivan in the creation of the immortal 'Gilbert and Sullivan' operas.

For twenty-one years, Gilbert lived the life of a country squire at Grim's Dyke House, clearing the beautiful Harrow Weald Common of disorderly gypsies, founding a private menagerie on his estate, growing tropical fruit in the large hothouse that adjoined the mansion, making and swimming in a charming little artificial lake, and, after 1900, acting as a magistrate in one of the local courts.

Gilbert's happy life in the rural surroundings of Harrow Weald came to a sudden end on 29 May, 1911. He had lunched at a club in London on that day and afterwards had visited May Fortescue, the actress, who had been thrown from her horse in Hyde Park and was laid up. Then, he caught a train from Marylebone to Harrow, where he met two young women with whom he had arranged to swim. He drove them by car to Grim's Dyke, and the girls were soon splashing about happily in the water of Gilbert's artificial lake. Neither of Gilbert's guests could swim well, however, and one of them—Ruby Preece—suddenly found herself in difficulties. As the older girl reported afterwards:

> . . . It was a very hot day, but the water struck very cold. My pupil was a much better swimmer than I, and soon outdistanced me. We were both unaware that the lake was deep further out, and presently she tried to touch bottom and found herself out of her depth. She shrieked out, 'Oh, Miss Emery, I am drowning!' I called to Sir William, who was on the steps, and he called out to her not to be frightened, and that he was coming. He swam out to her very quickly, and I heard him say: 'Put your hands on my shoulders and don't struggle.' This she did, but almost immediately she called out that he had sunk under her hand and had not come up. We both called to him, but got no answer. I tried to reach them, but soon got out of my depth and could do nothing but call for help. My pupil managed to struggle to the bank, and presently the gardener came and got out the boat, but it seemed a long time before they recovered the body . . .

At the Coroner's inquest that followed, it was established that Gilbert had not drowned—he had died of heart failure caused, it seemed, by the sudden exertion called for by the gallant attempt at rescue.

CHAPTER THREE

The Boroughs of Brent and Barnet

THE London boroughs of Brent and Barnet include, within their boundaries, Wembley, Willesden, Hendon, Mill Hill and Totteridge, as well as several other suburbs whose names are not so widely known.

Until quite late in English history, Wembley was just part of Harrow, and was no larger than most isolated country hamlets. At the beginning of the nineteenth century the manor, which, in medieval times, had belonged to the Archbishops of Canterbury, was bought by a Mr. Gray. In 1810, Mr. Gray rebuilt the manor house and extended the park by which it was surrounded.

Later in the nineteenth century, as we have seen, the directors of the Metropolitan Railway Company pushed their lines resolutely outwards from London, bringing to and through the Wembley area their picturesque brown carriages which had the enticing slogan 'Live in Metroland' embossed on the door handles. Eventually, the Company acquired part of the well-timbered and agreeably undulating park that had been Mr. Gray's and set about converting it into a public pleasure ground that would be, the directors thought, the central amenity of the happy, profitable Metroland they were striving so hard to create.

The chief attraction of the railway company's park was to have been a mighty tower—the 'Watkin Tower'—named after Sir Edward Watkin, the Chairman of the Board. The directors intended that this tower should be nearly two hundred feet higher than the tower built for the Paris Exhibition of 1889 by Alexandre Gustave Eiffel, the celebrated French engineer. There were difficulties with drainage of the ground, however, and the tower was only two hundred feet high when the available funds ran out and the whole glorious project had to be given up. The first stage of the tower, known throughout Metroland as 'Watkin's Folly', was not finally dismantled until 1907.

In 1924, the pleasure grounds at Wembley became famous all

over the world when they were chosen as the site of the British Empire Exhibition. Most of the buildings that were put up to house this enormous trade show were taken down when the exhibition closed in the following year, but the Empire Stadium was left standing, and, since then, has been used to accommodate a great many national and international sporting events. In 1934, the Empire Pool was constructed near the stadium to cater for water sport enthusiasts, and these two great arenas were available, fourteen years later, as ready-made meeting places in which the first post-Second-World-War Olympic Games might be reasonably amicably fought out.

With so much going on in Wembley in the nineteen-twenties, thirties and forties, it is hardly surprising that the place became, during those three decades, a typically modern and typically congested suburb of London. In most of the area now, unfortunately, one must expect to find roads and crescents laid out in a wholly unimaginative way, the uniformity of their widths and curvature emphasising the monotonous repetition of the semi-detached dwelling units, standardised in appearance and in specification, that they were designed to serve. It is hard to believe that any single person concerned with the construction of these uninspiring residences ever paused for a moment to consider, 'Now let me see, wasn't there something, once, called the Golden Section, or some such phrase as that?'

Willesden, a mile or two to the east of Wembley, was itself a country village until just over a century ago. Then the northbound railway lines were laid across the adjacent farmland, and the Metropolitan Railway reached rural Willesden Green. Today, Willesden is an area plentifully supplied with industrial undertakings that has lost almost all traces of its former pastoral beauty, and, in the remorseless expansion of the old village, has swallowed completely the charming neighbouring villages of Brondesbury, Dollis Hill, Dudden Hill, Harlesden, Kilburn, Mapesbury, Oxgate and Stonebridge. Kilburn has so many Irish residents, now, that some people would say it hardly qualifies to be considered as a suburb of London.

Immediately to the north of Willesden lies the L-shaped 'Welsh Harp' reservoir, formed in 1838 by the damming of the little River Brent as it made its way down to the Thames. The reservoir got its name from the public house on its banks, to which, for several decades, Londoners flocked on high days and holidays for careless enjoyment. The reservoir is still used for dinghy sailing and other small-scale water sports and is, as a contemporary guide book reports, 'a pretty sight at week-ends'.

At the beginning of the eighteenth century, the land round Hendon was held by William, Marquis of Powis, last of the long line of Herberts who had been Lords of the Manor ever since the Dissolution of the Monasteries in 1536. Up to the time of the Marquis' death 'without issue' in 1748, the district was predominantly agricultural, but it started to change its character entirely after 1756, when the manor was sold by order of His Late Lordship's executors. It was bought by a Mr. Clutterbuck on behalf of the celebrated actor David Garrick. Garrick thereupon built a new house for himself, calling it 'Hendon Hall' and using for the portico a set of great columns he had purchased from the Chandos' break-up sale at Canons. In spite of his noble intentions, Garrick was not entirely able to sustain the grand manner, however, and soon the demesne lands were being divided up and sold to families whose heads needed to make their livings in London, but who wished to find in rural Hendon their meed of peace and seclusion.

The second great change in the character of Hendon came about largely as a result of the activities of Mr. Claude Grahame-White.

When this great pioneer was born in 1879, Hendon was still a pretty village, a little too far from London to attract visitors. As late as 1908, someone sending a picture postcard from Hendon was able to write on the back, 'It's quite like country out here. 30 minutes to nearest shop so cannot spend much.' The front of the card showed a picturesque group of old cottages, shaded by lofty and undiseased elms, and a blacksmith's forge referred to as 'Suckling's'.

In 1909, Grahame-White, who owned one of the first petrol-driven cars to be seen in England, and had started a small but successful motor-engineering business in Albemarle Street in London's West End, became interested in the new science of aeronautics. Before that year was out, he had been granted a certificate of proficiency as an aviator—he was the first Englishman to achieve this distinction—and he had started a school of aviation at Pau, in France, which is usually referred to as the first British flying school.

In 1910, the proprietors of the *Daily Mail* newspaper offered a prize of £10,000 (then, a very large sum) to be won by the first person to make an aeroplane flight from London to Manchester. The successful flier, they stipulated, should pass within five miles of their offices.

On 21 April, Grahame-White made his first attempt to win the prize. After taking off from Wormwood Scrubs, in West London, he flew for some eighty-three miles and landed not far from Rugby. After an hour's rest there, he took off again, but after covering a total of 117 miles he was brought down near Lichfield, in Staffordshire, by a combination of high winds and engine trouble. His machine was damaged by the winds while it was still on the ground, and he was unable to continue the flight.

Meanwhile, the French aviator Monsieur Paulhan had arrived in England with the intention of winning the prize. On 27 April, Paulhan took off from a suitably open space at Hendon—the place had been suggested by some flying enthusiasts who lived in the vicinity—and he flew direct to Lichfield as the first stage of his trip. When Grahame-White heard that his rival was in the air and heading for Manchester he took off once again from Wormwood Scrubs and set out in pursuit.

About an hour later, when he was still only about sixty miles from the Scrubs, Grahame-White was forced to come down, as darkness was falling. He knew that Paulhan was already quite a long way ahead of him. He knew, too, that his own machine was considerably slower than Paulhan's. So, he decided that he would take just a short rest and, after that, would fly on through the night, guided as far as possible by the headlights of cars, or by any lights that he might be lucky enough to see on the railways.

As dawn broke, Grahame-White was still flying, but once again strong winds were to force him down. This time, his machine came to earth just ten miles from the bit of sheltered ground on which Paulhan had spent a comparatively restful night. As the skies grew lighter in the east, Paulhan heaved the foreign aircraft into the air again. Before Grahame-White had had a proper chance to catch up with what was happening, Paulhan had reached Manchester and had been awarded the prize.

And that might have been that, as far as Grahame-White was concerned, if he had not been rushed quickly into the rôle of a popular hero. In the next few months, he was invited to demonstrate his skill at 'flying meetings' in many different places in the

British Isles, and at a few places in America. When he returned to his native country at the end of the year, he took a very shrewd look at the meadows in Hendon from which his rival in the great race had ascended. Then, guided possibly by some Freudian desire to compensate for the disappointment of his defeat, he bought them and proceeded to convert them into a permanently established flying ground.

From then on, Hendon and flying became, in the minds of Londoners, almost synonymous. Saturday after Saturday, in those halcyon days before the First World War, little crowds of visitors would make their way out through the seemingly endless cornfields to Grahame-White's primitive 'aerodrome'. In an article published in the *Hendon and Finchley Times*, a Mr. Warden, who was a boy then, has recalled the scene:

> Flying was still something wonderful and those Saturday afternoons around the aerodrome will long be remembered . . . The pioneers . . . thrilled the spectators simply by rising in the air and when the loop was first looped over Hendon it was regarded as the most daring performance that had ever been seen . . . Seated in little groups one took tea and watched the evolutions. It was an agreeable way of passing an idle hour in which there was sure to be some exciting incident. For aeroplanes used to fall at that time fairly frequently. They could not be relied upon to remain in the air and nasty landings were common . . .

Grahame-White's friends thought that by buying so much Hendon land, he was letting himself in for financial disaster. In spite of their gloomy prognostications, the aviator's confidence in his great venture was at first fully justified. In the first twelve months alone, the gate receipts at his flying field totalled £11,000, and this sum increased year by year. Soon, a bus service had to be organised, to help intending visitors to reach the 'airport', and the village of Hendon, which had started to expand, swelled suddenly to become a good-sized town. The aerodrome, correspondingly, became one of the best-known and most competently organised flying grounds in the world, and the flying displays and aerial contests held there were events rated almost as highly in the social calendar as the race meetings at Ascot and Epsom. With the arrival of the Airco Company at The Hyde, nearby, the De Havilland Company at Stag Lane and the Handley Page Company's move, in 1917, from

Barking to Cricklewood, North London became the principal centre, in England, of the aircraft industry.

Grahame-White's run of good fortune lasted through the First World War. When that war broke out, his company at Hendon was engaged in building aircraft in quite a small way, only twenty people being employed in this branch of its activities. The company, then, went into full production, Grahame-White himself being allowed to relinquish his commission in the Royal Naval Air Service so that he could concentrate on the task of building planes and training pilots to fly them. By the end of the war, three thousand people were hard at work in the factory.

Then disaster struck. Just before it became clear that Germany was going to capitulate, the company at Hendon had been given orders for hundreds of aircraft. When it was seen that these would no longer be needed, the Air Ministry cancelled the contracts. Grahame-White, finding himself as a consequence in real financial trouble, tried to save the situation by switching the productive capacity of his plant to the manufacture of cars and furniture. The business did not prosper, however, and in 1922 the Treasury took possession of Grahame-White's Hendon factory and all the surrounding property and discharged his staff and employees. A long legal battle followed, as a result of which the Air Ministry assumed control of the aerodrome after agreeing to pay a large sum of money as compensation to Grahame-White.

So, the old meadows at Hendon became an important Royal Air Force station, and they continued to fulfil that function for several years, during which the place was used for more thrilling and historic air displays. Eventually, however, the increasing size and speed of military and other aircraft and the rapidly increasing rate of house building around Hendon made the place quite unsuitable for intensive air activity. The aerodrome had a short revival of life during the Second World War, when it was used briefly as a first line flying station—Winston Churchill made a dramatic journey to France from there, in 1940, and five years later Count Bernadotte flew from Hendon on his armistice mission to the German High Command—but this flurry of activity soon died, and within ten years of the end of the war, flying at Hendon had virtually ceased. The old aerodrome has recently been made available for 'development' and thousands of houses have been built or are being built on it, but the ground's associations with the early days of flying are commemorated by the name that has been given to the area—the 'Grahame Park Estate'—and by the new Royal Air Force Museum, built on the site of the Pavilion of the old Flying Club.

In spite of all the hectic building that has been going on, during the past few decades, in what is now the London Borough of Barnet, there are a few places that have managed to retain some of their old 'country village' atmosphere.

There is the charming little area known as 'Church End', for instance, which lies immediately around the thirteenth-century parish church. Here, near the top of the evocatively named Greyhound Hill, stands the Greyhound public house where, in a building that formerly occupied the site, the meetings of the parish council used to be held. Near the old inn, and just a little way down the hill from it, is Church Farm House, a delightful building that dates from the middle of the seventeenth century and is now maintained as a museum of local history, the ground floor being arranged and furnished much as it might have been in the eighteenth or early nineteenth centuries.

A little more than a mile to the north of Church End is Mill Hill, another of the Hendon district's old villages, and beautifully sited on a long spur of high ground a little to the east of the busy Watford Way. Mill Hill is renowned, principally, for the school for boys that was founded in 1807, but there are several other very interesting buildings in the neighbourhood—among them, Highwood House, which was for a time the home of Sir Stamford Raffles (1781–1826), the explorer who established the modern city of Singapore. An earlier house that stood on the same site was the home of Lord William Russell, who was beheaded in 1683 for the part he played in the Rye House conspiracy. The well that Lord William's wife Lady Rachel had constructed for her daughter's use is still in existence today.

Totteridge, north-east of Mill Hill, is one of the most picturesque village-suburbs of London, as it contains some splendid houses built in the eighteenth century by men prominent in the City of London who expected that everything they owned should be the last epitome of elegance.

Monken Hadley, three miles to the north, is equally delightful. This old village is believed by many authorities to be the true scene of the Battle of Barnet, fought in the early hours of the morning of

Easter Sunday, 1471. Long before noon, on that bloody Sunday, the Earl of Warwick ('The Kingmaker') was lying dead, with some fifteen hundred other ex-combatants, on Hadley Green, and on the ground beyond, which is still sometimes referred to as 'Dead Man's Bottom'. The village of Monken Hadley, today, has been designated a 'conservation area', which means that it will be protected, as far as it is possible to do so, from those who may wish to spoil its rare beauty and tranquil atmosphere.

CHAPTER FOUR

Hampstead and Highgate

STRETCHING themselves invitingly along the skyline just to the north of London, and only an hour or two's horsedrawn travel away, the well-wooded slopes of Hampstead and Highgate have offered the citizens of the metropolis, for some centuries, almost irresistible opportunities for pleasure and relaxation. They still have a potent appeal today.

Hampstead first became one of London's favourite pleasure resorts in the gay days that followed the Restoration of the Monarchy. Then, the chalybeate springs near the village became well known for their medicinal qualities. Crowds flocked to the wells on the Northern Heights to take the waters, and for those who were unable to make the journey to Hampstead, the owners of the rival springs sent consignments of the water every morning down to London. One advertised: 'The Chalybeate Waters at Hampstead, being of the same nature and equal in virtue with Tunbridge Wells. Sold by Mr. Richard Philps, Apothecary, at the Eagle and Child in Fleet Street, every morning at 3 pence per flask; and conveyed to persons at their own houses for one penny per flask more. The flask to be returned daily . . .'

Like most of the other fashionable watering places of the time, Hampstead became in the early eighteenth century the resort of 'the wealthy, the idle and the sickly'. A comedy called *Hampstead Heath*, which was played to large and enthusiastic audiences at the Drury Lane Theatre in 1706 contained this description, spoken by the girl called 'Arabella': 'Well, this Hampstead's a charming place—to dance all night at the Wells, and be treated at Mother Huff's—to have presents made one at the Raffling-shops, and then take a walk in Cane Wood with a man of wit that's not over-rude . . .'

In the opinion of most of the people who live there, Hampstead has remained a charming place, and attempts to alter the character of the old village, with its steep roads and by-lanes, meet with little sympathy. So, parts of Hampstead have not changed much since the days when John Keats lived, wrote and suffered there.

Keats became a student at the medical school of St. Thomas's and Guy's Hospitals in 1815. By that time, he had already started to write poetry, some of which had been read and admired by Leigh Hunt who was living, then, in the Vale of Health. Two years later, encouraged probably by Hunt, Keats and his brothers went to lodge at a cottage in Well Walk. The cottage has now disappeared, but the house where he lived, later, in John Street is still standing, and can be visited. (Since 1920, the street in which it stands has been re-named 'Keats Grove'.) The time Keats spent at this house was all too short, for the dreaded consumption was rapidly killing him. As a writer in *Hone's Table Book* of 1827 recorded: 'Winding southwardly from the heath, there is a charming little grove in Well Walk, with a bench at the end; whereon I last saw poor Keats, the poet of the "Pot of Basil", sitting and sobbing his dying breath into a handkerchief—glancing parting looks towards the quiet landscape he had delighted in—musing as in his Ode to a Nightingale . . .' Coleridge, meeting the young poet out walking, pressed his hand and observed, afterwards, to someone who was walking with him, 'There is death in that hand'. Keats died in Rome on 23 February, 1821.

Hampstead Heath—over eight hundred acres of unspoiled land—has been for centuries a great place for Londoners to go for pleasure of various kinds on bank holidays and at week-ends. That being so, it is hardly surprising that the immediate neighbourhood of the Heath is exceptionally well supplied with very good hotels and public houses. 'The Spaniards', which stands by the road that leads to Highgate, is believed to have been opened early in the seventeenth century by a man who had left the service of the Spanish Ambassador. (The natives found his name too hard to pronounce.) The house was patronised occasionally by Charles Dickens. He liked it well enough to make it, in his *Pickwick Papers*, the resort of Mrs. Bardell and her cronies.

The great novelist went more often to 'Jack Straw's Castle', which stands at one of the highest points of the Heath. (The present building, which replaces the older inn that was badly damaged during the Second World War, is nearly 450 feet above sea level.) This beautifully situated pub is supposed to have derived its name from the Jack Straw who was Wat Tyler's second-in-command in the great rebellion of 1381, and who is believed to have lived in a hovel on the site. There is a tradition, too, that the old inn was much used by the numerous highwaymen who operated on the Heath. In the car park, visitors can see an iron ring to which Dick Turpin is said to have tethered his famous mare Black Bess.

On the sloping ground behind Jack Straw's Castle, the corpse of John Sadleir, Member of Parliament for Sligo, was found on the morning of Sunday, 17 February, 1856. Beside the body of the unfortunate man, who had got himself into hopeless financial difficulties, there was a phial of poison and a silver cream jug from which Sadleir had taken the fatal draught. The Lord of the Manor of Hampstead at that time happened to possess some very extensive rights, among them the right of 'deodand'. By this ancient privilege, the Lord of the Manor became entitled, in the case of any person who committed suicide in his territory, to 'the whole of the goods and chattels of the deceased, of every kind, with the exception of his estate of inheritance, in the event of a jury returning a verdict of *felo de se*'. Poor Sadleir had not many goods or chattels left that were worth taking, but the Lord of the Manor formally claimed, and received, the silver cream jug as an acknowledgment of his dues before he passed it back to the M.P.'s executors.

Around Hampstead Heath, there are some of the finest mansions to be seen in the London area. Kenwood House, which was remodelled for Lord Mansfield by Robert Adam in the years after 1764, is one of the most palatial, but there are also such delightful smaller places as Fenton House, which belongs to the National Trust and can be visited on any day except Tuesdays. Inside Fenton House there are splendid collections of furniture and porcelain and the rare and serviceable keyboard instruments given to the National Trust in 1937 by the late Major G. H. Benton-Fletcher.

Near the Heath, too, there are two quite remarkable suburban developments—the Holly Lodge Estate and the Hampstead Garden Suburb. Holly Lodge was the home of Angela Burdett-Coutts, who was the granddaughter of Thomas Coutts, the great banker. Enormously wealthy, Miss Burdett-Coutts spent much of her time doing philanthropic work on behalf of the poorer people of London and was made a Baroness in her own right by Queen Victoria in recognition of her good deeds. She founded 'Holly

Village' in 1865 to provide accommodation for her workpeople in Gothic cottages situated round a 'village green'.

It is quite possible that there would be no such place as Hampstead Garden Suburb today if John Ruskin, the nineteenth-century art critic and social reformer, had not offered to teach Miss Octavia Hill how to draw. Miss Hill, the eighth daughter of a merchant and banker, accepted Ruskin's invitation, and out of her visits to his home grew the first of her housing schemes: a development in a slum court in Marylebone. Ruskin put up the money: she was to manage the property. She did this so successfully that soon a Society of Women Housing Managers was brought into being, so that her ideas could be widely disseminated.

Miss Hill was an extremely busy woman. Besides being involved with her housing projects, she pioneered the Open Space Movement, was one of the principal founders of the National Trust, and organised the first Cadet Corps for lads. To help her with her 'Charity Organisation Society' Miss Hill secured the services of a slightly younger woman, Miss Henrietta Rowland, youngest of the eight children of a well-to-do merchant. Miss Rowland's particular duties involved the supervision of the work done by the occupants of the Society's properties. (It was so much more enlightened, to pay the poor for tasks done, than to hand out charitable 'doles'.)

Miss Rowland was just as idealistic and as energetic as Miss Hill, but the two ladies differed in one important respect. Miss Hill believed that degraded people should be kept in disreputable conditions until they have proved themselves to be worthy of better ones. Miss Rowland believed that degraded people had to be put in a decent environment and kept there before they could know what a decent environment was like and would choose to strive towards it for themselves.

On 28 January, 1873 Miss Rowland married Samuel Barnett, an earnest young curate who was about to take up the living of St. Jude's, Whitechapel, which the Bishop of London at that time described as 'the worst parish in my diocese'. Looking back, in later life, the Reverend Barnett recalled the conditions that had prevailed in the parish when he and his wife first went to live there:

> There were two or three narrow streets lined with fairly decent cottages occupied entirely by Jews, but with these exceptions

> the whole parish was covered with a network of courts and alleys . . . None of these courts had roads. In some the houses were three storeys high and hardly six feet apart, the sanitary accommodation being pits in the cellars; in other courts the houses were lower, wooden and dilapidated, a standpipe at the end providing the only water. Each chamber was the home of a family who sometimes owned their indescribable furniture, but in most cases the rooms were let out furnished for 8d. a night . . . In many instances broken windows had been repaired with paper and rags, the banisters had been used for fire wood, and the paper hung from the walls which were the residence of countless vermin . . . If the men worked at all it was as casual dock labourers . . . Usually they did not work; they stole or received stolen goods, hawked, begged, cadged, lived on each other . . . drank, gambled, fought . . .

In 1884, the Reverend Barnett, Vicar of Whitechapel, founded Toynbee Hall—a do-good East-End-of-London Community Centre that is still doing an enormous amount of good today.

Five years after that, the Barnetts found that to retain their sanity, they would have to get away occasionally from the fearful squalor of the East End. Mrs. Barnett recalled, later: 'After we had lived a few years in Whitechapel we found it absolutely essential for health to get a Sabbath-day (which meant two nights) out of its noise and dirt, and so we bought a house overlooking Hampstead Heath.'

The house, which they named 'St. Jude's Cottage', is today called 'Heath End House'. It is a white, weather-boarded three storey building that backs on to the 'Spaniards Inn'. When the Barnetts took it, it had a wonderful view over the eighteenth-century farmhouse known as 'Wylde's' and over the surrounding estate. Beyond that, the Barnetts could see over undulating Middlesex farmland as far as Hendon and Mill Hill.

The Barnetts were not to enjoy their priceless rural seclusion for long, though. Quite soon after they moved in, rumours started to circulate in the neighbourhood about an 'Underground Railway' which, said the chatterers, was to be constructed from London to Hampstead. Mrs. Barnett was shrewd enough to see that this railway, if it were made, would bring 'developments' of the very worst kind to the open areas beyond the Heath and that all too soon the ground round her beloved country retreat would be built on. Almost certainly, the houses that would spoil her views would be closely packed suburban 'villas' of a type that would be particularly repugnant to her—speculative dwellings like those that were blotting out the once green fields of Kilburn, Brondesbury and Willesden. The prospect was not a happy one.

In 1893, the Charing Cross, Euston and Hampstead Railway Company was incorporated by Act of Parliament, the intended terminus of the line being in Heath Street, Hampstead. A further Act passed in the following year gave the Company power to acquire additional lands. Further Acts were passed during the next few years that were designed to keep these options open and to extend them in various ways.

In 1896, the Reverend and Mrs. Barnett found out almost by accident where the line was likely to run when they met, on board a ship on which they were travelling to Russia, an American who told them that he happened to know. In 1900, the interest that Americans were taking in the project was confirmed when a Charles Tyson Yerkes, of New York, purchased the right to construct the Charing Cross-to-Hampstead Tube—paying, for the privilege, £100,000. In 1902, Yerkes consolidated the various investments he had made in London railways or potential railways, forming in the process the 'Underground Electric Railway Company'. From that moment, the construction of the Hampstead Tube was a practical proposition, since Yerkes had considerable financial backing from way back in the States. An Act of Parliament passed in November 1902 sanctioned the extension of the Hampstead Tube to Golders Green which, at that time, was a lonely crossroads with a solitary farm-house by it, entirely surrounded by fields.

Mrs. Barnett viewed the latest developments with alarm. The part of the plan that particularly worried her was a proposal that there should be an intermediate station—to be called, possibly, 'The Bull and Bush'—at North End, Hampstead, just by the beloved Wylde's Farmhouse.

By 9 May, 1903, Canon Barnett (the Reverend had been made, by that time, a Canon of Bristol, his home town) was writing to his brother: 'My wife has added to her cares by trying to save the neighbouring fields from the builders. She wants a millionaire . . .' Mrs. Barnett did not get her philanthropic millionaire—such people were scarcer then than they are today—but she had plenty of influential friends, and she was extraordinarily astute. Her aims were simple. As she put it, inarguably, 'there was nothing else to do but enlarge the Heath'.

To achieve her simple and entirely worthy aims, Mrs. Barnett, helped by her husband, convened a committee, which she called, grandly, the 'Hampstead Heath Extension Council'. So that the Local Authority should be kept informed of what she was up to, Mrs. Barnett told the members of the Hampstead Borough Council that a scheme 'based on a business footing' was being prepared, with the object of purchasing from the Eton College Trustees eighty acres of the Wylde's Farm Estate. Mrs. Barnett later paid a public tribute to all those who assisted her in her dynamic and entirely unselfish campaign: 'Those who did the seemingly interminable work of addressing envelopes, folding circulars, stamping letters (13,000 of them) which Miss Paterson [Mrs. Barnett's Secretary] and I signed . . . Those who organised and carried out street and shop collections . . . Who did accounts . . . Furnished lists . . . Made copies, got up drawing-room meetings . . . Headed deputations, addressed public meetings . . . Accomplished all the dull out-of-sight work . . .'

Mrs. Barnett's money-raising efforts were phenomenally successful. Her final list of subscribers filled nine and a half pages, their names being arranged in two columns on each page. The most generous donors right at the top of Page One were the members of the London County Council who, at first, were reluctant to subscribe at all. (Hampstead, the good councillors said, was a rich suburb and had an unusually large number of open spaces already.) After further determined prodding from the importunate Mrs. Barnett, they handed over £8,000 of their ratepayers' money. A 'Master Crump and Friend', at the bottom of the list, contributed a welcome shilling that came, presumably, from their own little pockets.

Mrs. Barnett's scheme for enlarging Hampstead Heath did not meet with unqualified approval in every quarter, however. Several members of the local Borough Council, led by a Councillor Lyell, felt that the extension of the Heath by another eighty acres would keep working-class dwellers at a greater distance from the traditional pleasure ground and would therefore benefit the richer residents of Hampstead at the expense of the poor. They did not like the idea at all.

Needing the whole-hearted support of the Borough Council for her schemes, Mrs. Barnett then had to sit back and think up another. Her new project involved all the rest of the Wylde's Farm Estate—243 acres of it, extending beyond the farm north-west to the Finchley Road. Hampstead, she knew, had a housing problem, like most of the other London boroughs of the time. Why should not the remaining Wylde's Farm ground be used for a garden suburb 'for the industrial classes'? In a letter to the *Hampstead and Highgate Express*, Mrs. Barnett explained the advantages of her plan, which was to establish: 'Not . . . a "garden city", but a "garden suburb", in which every house, however humble, will be surrounded by a garden large enough to be productive as well as pleasurable. The plan . . . will necessitate . . . shops . . . and some houses of larger size . . .'

It took Mrs. Barnett and the other members of her Council a considerable time to raise the money and to carry out all the legal arrangements for the purchase of the land, and for making over the Heath Extension to the London County Council. In the meantime, the construction of the Underground Railway had been continuing apace, and work on the dreaded station on the North End site was already well advanced 'in anticipation of considerable housing development in the immediate vicinity'. With the extension of the Heath, however, the prospects for the station became dim, as the number of passengers who would be likely to use it would not justify the necessary expenditure and maintenance, so it was never finished. (The plot of ground on which the station entrance was to have been constructed was sold in 1927 and the house known as 'One Hampstead Way' was built on part of the site. Ghost platforms, nearby, remind those who know the story of the successful outcome of Mrs. Barnett's anti-Tube campaign.)

The suburb 'for the industrial classes' that Mrs. Barnett had dreamed up was intended, from the start, to be as unlike squalid Whitechapel as she could possibly make it. The houses were to be designed for the working poor by the very best architects that Mrs. Barnett could interest in her scheme. Sir Raymond Unwin, who was principally responsible for the original layout and who wanted to give the suburb an identity as distinct as that of the medieval villages that had been absorbed into the built-up area of London, and Edwin Lutyens, who laid out Central Square and designed many of the buildings round it, were only two of the distinguished contributors who fell victims to the spell of the indomitable Mrs. Barnett.

And, there were the all-important gardens. In an article she wrote in 1905 for the *Contemporary Review*, Mrs. Barnett pointed out that Mr. Cadbury, of the 'Bournville' estate, had testified that his tenants, who each had a garden of just under an eighth of an acre, had made 'an average profit of 1s. 11½d. a week, a material reduction of house rents which vary from 5s. 6d. to 8s. 6d. a week'. Of the ethical value of working in gardens, Mr. Cadbury had written: 'The benefit, physically, morally and even spiritually is so great that it would have been worth while cultivating the gardens even if there had been no profit from the labour expended.'

So, Mrs. Barnett decided, the houses in *her* suburb should be arranged so that whenever a resident looked from a window he would see something green and growing and would therefore be protected from the temptations of such morally destructive activities as drinking and gambling. (There was a theory, fashionable in some intellectual circles at the time, that honest toil on the land was of itself a good and moral thing which kept working men away from sin. Mrs. Barnett believed it implicitly.) On 2 March, 1909 she wrote, in her capacity as Honorary Manager of the Hampstead Garden Suburb Trust Limited, to every incoming tenant saying that she had been able to buy some apple trees, some small-leaved climbing ivy and some purple clematis, and asked: 'Would you like me to instruct the Estate gardener to plant one of each of the latter in the front of your house, and the apple tree in the garden? I know it is not usual to present tenants with gifts but . . . we should all work together to make our Suburb really a *garden* one . . .'

There is little doubt that Mrs. Barnett's attitude to the splendid garden suburb she was creating changed, almost imperceptibly, as her plans came to fruition. At first, she had intended that her houses should be for members of the industrial classes only. Then, she began to suspect that her suburb might be almost too good to be lavished on members of the working community alone. As her dream in its original form began to fade, its place was taken by another vision—her suburb should cater for a mixture of people. Persons of all classes of society should live there, as well as those of every level of income. By mixing with lords, she thought, the proles would learn what it was to live graciously. And so she justified the change.

There are not many proles living in Hampstead Garden Suburb today. Most of the residents regard it as a very special kind of place—a quiet and picturesque oasis set in a vast expanse of anonymous and unattractive suburbia. The overall income levels of the inhabitants of the suburb are much higher than the national average, and the houses change hands at prices that are almost prohibitive. Harold Wilson was living in the suburb when he became Prime Minister, and Rolls Royce cars are not uncommon in the streets.

Shortly before capital punishment was virtually abolished in Britain, there was an incident, in Hampstead, that profoundly influenced popular thinking on the subject. For two years, from 1953 to the early Spring of 1955, a young woman named Ruth Ellis had carried on a passionate love affair with a racing motorist called David Blakely. Mrs. Ellis (she had been divorced), lived in a flat over a club of which she was the manageress, but in February, 1955 the couple tried living together at an apartment in Egerton Gardens in Kensington. The experiment was not entirely successful and there were a number of quarrels. At last, when the rows became particularly unpleasant, Blakely moved out.

On 8 April, 1955, which was Good Friday, Mrs. Ellis went to Hampstead where, she knew, Blakely was due to spend the weekend with friends who lived in Tanza Road. When she called at the house, and was refused admittance, she made such an uproar that the police had to be fetched and asked to take her away.

On the evening of that Easter Sunday, Ruth Ellis went back to the house in Tanza Road. From inside there came sounds that suggested to her that a party might be taking place on the premises. Shortly before 9 p.m., Blakely left the house with a female companion, and the pair made their way to the nearby 'Magnolia' public house. When they left the 'Magnolia', Ruth Ellis, who had been waiting outside, drew a gun and shot her ex-lover dead. She was tried at the Old Bailey, found guilty of murder, sentenced to death, and hanged.

Highgate, which lies to the east of Hampstead Heath, owes its name to a medieval toll gate. By 1300, the Old North Road of the Romans—'Ermine Street'—had been largely superseded by a road that lay a little to the west of it. When this newer road became almost impassable, the citizens of London suggested that they should cut an entirely new road, that would pass directly over the eastern spur of the Northern Heights, crossing incidentally lands over which their Bishop held the manorial rights. The Bishop agreed to the proposition, but he shrewdly insisted that he should be allowed to build and operate a toll gate at the summit. Around this levying point there developed the village of 'High Gate'.

Highgate is not nearly as picturesque or as charming as Hampstead, though it does contain a few handsome houses. The village will be associated for all time with the runaway apprentice Richard Whittington, who, it is said, was resting there in a weary and footsore state when he heard Bow bells chiming a message to him sweetly from their belfry in the valley far below: 'Turn again, Whittington, Thrice Lord Mayor of London Town'. Reassured, the boy went back to London with his cat. (This makes a telling scene in the traditional Christmas pantomime.) He did become Lord Mayor of London—in 1397, 1406 and 1419—and left a vast fortune. His connection with Highgate is commemorated by the two taverns that have been called after him, by the Whittington almshouses founded from his wealth, and by 'Pauntley Street', which gets its name from the village in Gloucestershire from which the boy first came to London, seeking a fortune.

The nineteenth-century Church of St. Michael, at Highgate, stands on ground that was once partly covered by Arundel House, one of the homes of Thomas Howard, Second Earl of Arundel. Here, in 1626, died Francis Bacon, one of the most brilliant and learned of all England's Lord Chancellors, whose most valuable contribution to the advancement of science lay in his unique perception of the greatness and variety of Nature. John Aubrey, the antiquary, recorded in these words the cause of Bacon's death:

> Mr. Hobbs told me that the cause of his Lordship's death was trying an experiment, viz., as he was taking the Aire in a coach with Dr. Witherborne (a Scotchman, Physitian to the King), towards Highgate, snow lay on the ground, and it came into my Lord's thought, why flesh might not be preserved in snow, as in salt. They were resolved they would try the experiment presently. They alighted out of the coach and went into a poore woman's house at the bottom of Highgate Hill, and bought a Hen, and made the woman extenterate [disembowel] it, and

then stuffed the body with Snow, and my Lord did helpe to doe it himselfe. The snow so chilled him that he immediately felt so extremely ill that he could not returne to his lodgings (I suppose then at Graye's Inne), but went to the Earl of Arundel's house at Highgate, where they put him into a good bed warmed with a Panne, but it was a damp bed that had not been layn-in about a year before . . .

Sir Francis caught pneumonia from his rest in the unaired bed, and he died in the arms of his kinsman, Sir Julius Caesar, a few days later. Just before he expired, he dictated a letter to his absent host in which he said that the housekeeper had been 'very careful and diligent' and that 'Your Lordship's house was happy to me'. Later in that century, the house changed hands two or three times. Then, part of it was demolished and rebuilt, to form 'The Old Hall', which is still lived in, though now it is converted into flats.

Another historic Highgate residence that has survived, in part, lies a little to the east of The Old Hall. This is Lauderdale House, once the home of John Maitland, First Earl of Lauderdale, who was confined for some years in the Tower of London for the powerful support he gave to the Royalist cause in the Civil War. Samuel Pepys called on the Lauderdales at Highgate in July 1666 and found them, with some Scotch people, at supper. 'Pretty odd company', observed Pepys, adding: 'At supper there played one of their servants upon the viallin some Scotch tunes only . . . But, strange to hear my Lord Lauderdale say himself that he had rather hear a cat mew, than the best musique in the world; and the better the musique, the more sick it makes him; and that of all instruments, he hated the lute most, and, next to that the baggpipe . . .' There is a tradition that while Lauderdale was away in Scotland, King Charles II installed his mistress Nell Gwynne in the house. The remains of the mansion can be seen, now, in Waterlow Park.

Highgate has had many distinguished residents during its long history as one of London's most favoured suburbs. Literary figures who have elected to live on the east side of Hampstead Heath include Samuel Taylor Coleridge, who made his home at Number 3, The Grove during the last eighteen years of his life. (The room in which he died on 25 July, 1834 still exists, though the rest of that floor has been modernised by J. B. Priestley, who has occupied it in more recent years.) A. E. Housman lived from 1886 to 1905 at

Byron Cottage, 17 North Road, and while he was there wrote the well-loved collection of poems *A Shropshire Lad.* Sir John Betjeman's childhood home, 31 Highgate West Hill, has been celebrated memorably in the Poet Laureate's *Summoned by Bells.*

Behind St. Michael's Church lies Highgate Cemetery, where Karl Marx was buried in 1883, having spent the last twenty-seven years of his life not far away, in St. Pancras. Marx lies, a little incongruously, near Charles Dickens' improvident and ineffectual parents, who were depicted so vividly in *David Copperfield* as 'Mr. and Mrs. Micawber'. Other distinguished people who are buried in the cemetery at Highgate include Mary Ann Evans (the novelist 'George Eliot') and Christina Rossetti. Here, too, Lizzie Rossetti's body was exhumed, in 1869, so that the unpublished poems her distracted husband had placed in her coffin seven years earlier could be recovered. In recent years the old burying-ground has attracted the attention of students of witchcraft and other irreverent intruders.

CHAPTER FIVE

From Highgate to Enfield

A LITTLE to the east of Highgate, and just over the boundary of the London Borough of Hornsey, is an important road that was brought into full usefulness by a historic piece of civil engineering.

Archway Road was built so that travellers leaving London and making for the Great North Road could avoid the hazards of Highgate Hill. The project started in 1810, when a company was formed to make an alternative route to the steep, ancient north-bound track, with its awful surface, on which there were so many appalling accidents. Subscribers were found; the celebrated architects John Nash and John Rennie were retained as consultants; and a tunnel was started through the Hill that would be, when it was complete, nearly a hundred yards long. Before the excavations were finished, however, the roof of the tunnel fell in with a deafening roar. More money had to be collected from the unfortunate shareholders and thousands of tons of unwanted earth had to be shovelled away to form a steep-sided cutting through which the new road could pass as it was driven upwards at a fairly constant gradient.

The road, when it was finished, looked really handsome, with its pilastered entrance lodges and its carefully tended banks, but in rainy weather it acted as a sluice, and for a good part of the year it was flooded so often that it was reckoned to be practically impassable. Then, in 1829, Thomas Telford was called in to give advice, and he completely revised the systems of drainage, so that the road remained reasonably dry even in the depths of winter. The viaduct that had to be built to carry the old Hornsey Lane over the new road became, almost as soon as it was open, internationally famous as the place from which the great city of London could be most satisfactorily viewed. (When Hans Christian Andersen was invited to England to stay with Charles Dickens, the revered Danish writer was taken across the viaduct in the dark by his host, and saw 'the great world metropolis mapped out in fire below him'.) Less happily, the Archway viaduct also became known, like the City's Monument and the Pagoda at Kew, as a very convenient place from which unhappy people might commit suicide. So many desperate souls jumped to destruction off it, during the 'Hungry Forties', that railings seven feet high had to be erected along its sides. This may have made the Viaduct somewhat safer, but it certainly did not improve its appearance.

Just to the east of Highgate is Hornsey—an old borough that has been absorbed, since 1965, in the London Borough of Haringey. Most of Hornsey was forest ground until comparatively late in the Middle Ages. The first settlement in the district probably consisted of a few houses and cottages clustered round old St. Mary's church, the tower of which is still standing, and the Bishop of London is known to have had a hunting lodge at Lodge Hill.

Then, when the trees around were gradually felled, their timber being required for new buildings in the cities of London and Westminster, or for firing, the rich started to put up mansions on the cleared ground (Sir Julius Caesar, Master of the Rolls to King James I, had a splendid residence called 'Mattysons' at Muswell Hill) and a number of picturesque small villages such as Crouch End, Fortis Green and Stroud Green came into being. With the coming of the railways the Great Northern Railway's station at Hornsey was opened in 1860; and other lines reached Crouch End and Highgate in 1867, Finsbury Park in 1869, Muswell Hill in 1873 and Stroud Green in 1881—the countryside inevitably began to disappear, and the villages were absorbed in a suburban sprawl that is relieved, here, only by such open spaces as Highgate and Queen's Woods and Priory Park.

Between Muswell Hill and another old village—Wood Green—is the high ridge on which stands one of North London's most dominating landmarks, the Alexandra Palace. This great structure was intended, in the first instance, to house exhibitions and to provide entertainment for the people of North London as the 'Crystal Palace' at Sydenham did for the South Londoners. As a writer in a mid-Victorian newspaper put it:

> It has long been felt as a sort of grievance by the North Londoners that their distance from the Crystal Palace was so serious an obstacle as almost to preclude them from visiting that world-renowned structure. Paterfamilias, in order to encompass the

desired object, had to rouse all his faculties to shew himself equal to the occasion. For days before elaborate plans had to be laid, railways maps inspected, the merits and defects of the various lines discussed, and finally, when the most desirable route had been selected among the network of lines through which the life of the busiest city in the world pulsates in its ever ceaseless ebb and flow, last, not least, came the question of expenditure, when every item was carefully estimated and balanced to prevent the catastrophe which a deficit would produce . . .

The Alexandra Palace was opened to the public on 24 May, 1873, a new branch railway having been constructed from the Great Northern Line to bring passengers directly to the beautifully laid out grounds. The first visitors wandered amazed through the luxuriously appointed building, described by a contemporary observer as 'the splendid and capacious structure on Muswell Hill, the youngest born of London's gigantic enterprises for the recreation of the multitude'. A few found the richness of the palace's interiors a little overpowering. 'Whatever the ornamental or decorative features of a building of this kind may be', wrote one critic, 'the great attractions lie in the lighter entertainments which are provided. Expensive courts imitating the gorgeous palaces reared in ancient or medieval time undoubtedly have their influence in encouraging a taste for the fine arts, but to the general public, who are wofully indifferent to such considerations, too much art has the contrary effect to that wished by the designers, and repels the very persons for whom these buildings are supposed to be constructed.'

Not many persons were repelled, however. For two glorious weeks the public flocked in, at least 124,000 visitors paying for admission during that time.

Then, 'Alas'—and the quotation comes directly from *The Times* newspaper—'an appalling catastrophe befell the splendid and capacious structure on Muswell Hill.' 'We are almost tempted to believe', wrote the *Thunderer* 'that the Fire King intended to assert his dread supremacy in our waning belief in his power and to show, by a terrible and tremendous blow our utter futility in the face of his over-mastering strength . . .'

The great conflagration started in the broad blaze of noonday, when there were only five hundred or so persons in the palace. (Had the fire broken out during the previous week-end, which was Whitsun, there might well have been appalling carnage.) As it was, the five hundred or so persons, 'free from the mad infectious terror of a surging crowd, behaved in the most admirable manner . . . Amid the lurid glare which began to overspread the roof, and the warning cackle of the gathering flames, the building was quietly evacuated without disorder or confusion.'

A rush was made to the hydrants, reported *The Times*, 'and if the pressure had been adequate to raise the water to the burning roof, some good effect might have followed the exertions of the firemen'. Unfortunately, though, the palace had to suffer the consequences of being in such a lofty and commanding position as the fire-fighters found it impracticable to obtain a fresh supply of water owing to the contour of the ground:

> In less than half-an-hour after the first alarm had been given, the whole interior was one dense seething mass of fire, belching forth huge lambent tongues of flame, and surmounted by black whirling columns of smoke, which seen from afar towered high above the horizon, and became a conspicuous object for miles around. At half past one the gigantic ribs, twelve in number, sustaining the roof, fell with a hideous crash, the reverberation being distinctly heard within a circuit of six miles; and carrying with them the glowing incandescent mass which was all that remained of the great central dome. The great organ and the orchestral amphitheatre were at the same time crushed beneath the immense mass of falling debris. The flames feeding on the combustible materials of which the Palace was composed raged with such unintermittent fury that before two o'clock not a vestige of the roof or the upper walls, except the eight gable entrances, remained standing. When the steam engines, which arrived under Captain Shaw, together with the village engines, and two engines sent by special train from King's Cross were on the spot, the Palace no longer existed . . .

A singular scene was presented outside the blackened shell of the building, where a motley assortment of quaint but almost priceless tapestries, paintings by Turner, and other objects of lesser value that had been plucked from the burning lay jumbled higgledy-piggledy together on the grass: 'The grotesquely habited figures, with their placid staring features, and the miscellaneous wreckage which represented the china and glass ware of Messrs. Bertram and Roberts, melted and distorted into every conceivable shape, lay mingled with the toys and jewellery and the masterpieces of the artist', observed the man from *The Times*.

Encouraged by the number of people who had visited the palace during the short time it had been open, the directors decided almost at once to get back into business. So, they built a new palace, with a Great Hall that would be suitable for the performance of orchestral and choral works, and it was completed and opened to the public together with an adjoining race course in 1875. The enterprise was not entirely successful from the financial point of view, so, in 1900, seven of the neighbouring local authorities agreed to purchase the building, with the whole of its grounds, each authority contributing a share of the cost. The palace looked really dilapidated by 1935, but it earned a new lease of life in that year when part of it was taken by the British Broadcasting Corporation for use as Britain's first television transmitting centre. By the time the Corporation started to build its own Television Centre at Lime Grove, Shepherds Bush, the revenues the broadcasters had contributed had enabled the trustees to renovate many parts of the buildings. The palace, today, is used principally for exhibitions, 'pop' music concerts, and the examinations of the Law Society and other public bodies. There is even a ski-slope in its grounds.

Wood Green, a little to the east of the Alexandra Palace, originated as a small settlement in a clearing at the side of the heavily wooded manor of Tottenham. There was a public grazing ground in the middle of the hamlet, and from this little common the place derived its original name 'Tottenham Wode Green'. By 1798, the population of Wood Green had risen to one hundred, and as at that date the place proudly possessed an inn ('The Three Jolly Butchers'), a forge and a shop, it could properly qualify to be referred to as a village. The building of a railway station at Wood Green in 1859 soon led to the place changing from a village to an extensive residential town. Now, Wood Green has been selected by the Greater London Council for development as a 'major strategic centre', which means that it will be blessed with vast traffic-free shopping precincts, piped music, multi-storey car parks, and numerous other up-to-date urban amenities.

Tottenham, as mentioned above, was a well-wooded manor in the Middle Ages. It was also a very lordly place, belonging, in its time, to Judith, niece of William the Conqueror, then to her daughter Maud, who was married to the King of Scotland and eventually, in part, to the family of Robert the Bruce. (Their share of Tottenham was taken back from the Bruces by King Edward II in 1306, when Robert threw in his lot with forces hostile to the English crown.)

On the east side of the manor, the land sloped down to the wide marshy flats through which oozed the flood-prone River Lea. When banks were thrown up so that the river might be contained, and the surrounding marshes were drained, a great new London-to-Cambridge road was constructed on the west bank (the 'High Road', at Tottenham) and, after that, there was a constant traffic of kings and their armies passing north and south, through the manor. In 1516, it is recorded, King Henry VIII met his sister Margaret, Queen of Scotland, at 'Maister Compton's house beside Totnam'.

All through the eighteenth century and well into the nineteenth, Tottenham was one of the pleasantest villages within easy reach of London—the east side of the parish being largely owned by the Smithson family, one of whose members married the heiress of the Percy family and was created Duke of Northumberland in 1766. For a short time, even, after 1840, when Tottenham became connected to London when stations were built on the Great Eastern line at Northumberland Park and The Hale, the district kept its essentially rural quality, the persons helped principally by the newly developed form of transport being the market gardeners. The place was famous (as Sir John Betjeman has lovingly reminded us) for the cowslips and large-flowered forget-me-nots that grew in the old marshlands down by the Lea.

The real changes came with the opening of the Liverpool Street to Enfield line in 1872. Before they could construct this line, which involved the demolition of a large number of working-class homes on the outskirts of the City, the directors of the railway company had to agree to provide special trains for working men on which exceptionally low fares would be charged. By the 1880s, the Great Eastern Company was running a number of these trains to and from Enfield and Walthamstow, the charges on them being as little as 2d. return. Working-class suburbs, in consequence, sprang up all along the lines, and the character of the countryside was radically altered. As the manager of the company told a Royal Commission:

> Wherever you locate the workmen in large numbers you utterly destroy that neighbourhood for ordinary passenger traffic. Take, for instance, the neighbourhood of Stamford Hill, Tottenham and Edmonton. That used to be a very nice district indeed, occupied by good families, with houses of from £150 to £250 a year, with coach-houses and stables, and gardens, and a few acres of land. But very soon after this obligation was put upon the Great Eastern Company, and accepted by the Great Eastern Company, of issuing workmen's tickets, speculative builders went down into the neighbourhood and, as a consequence, each good house was one after another pulled down, and the district is given up entirely I may say now to the working man . . .

By 1931, there were more than 150,000 people living in Tottenham, and the figure has remained fairly steady since then. More than half the people who live there today rent their accommodation from some private landlord. For most of this century, rents have been held down, according to the national policy of helping poorer tenants. This has made it difficult for private landlords to meet their escalating repair bills. So, there is now in the area an unusually high proportion of run-down houses, houses where too much sharing takes place, and houses that are just not up to the standards required today. In some parts of Tottenham, where deep drifts of litter pile up, and where old motor cycles are cannibalised in tiny front 'gardens', one is reminded, regretfully, of a late Victorian slum.

But, there are other parts of this generally grim district that have managed to retain, in spite of all the difficulties, much of their old world charm. There is the area round All Hallows' Church, for instance. The church itself, which has an old flint tower topped with eighteenth-century bricks and an interior dramatically rejuvenated by William Butterfield during the nineteenth century, has been described by our Poet Laureate, Sir John Betjeman, as 'surprising, varied and beautiful'. The churchyard around it is surprising, varied and beautiful too, as it contains some splendid eighteenth-century tombs, carved from Portland stone, and many other handsome monuments. Unfortunately, insensitive vandals using the public footpath that runs through the churchyard have found it all too easy to desecrate the tombs and monuments so that some of them, now, are quite beyond repair. And, when the author of this book last visited the church, he found that its ancient west door had been painted by a crude anonymous hand with *graffiti* that were surprising and varied, but would hardly be called beautiful, even by someone with such a keen eye for the curious as the ever-receptive Sir John.

There is another historic building in Tottenham that is not very far from All Hallows' Church, but is much more carefully protected, because it happens to have found an up-to-date use as municipal offices. The name of this extraordinary pile is 'Bruce Castle'.

The early history of Bruce Castle is a little obscure, though it is known that for close on three centuries, prior to the year 1827, the castle was the country seat of the Lords of the Manor of Tottenham. In 1827, the patched-up and re-faced Tudor building was given an entirely new lease of life when it was purchased by a family from Birmingham and converted into a school. This family—the Hills—had been running 'progressive' educational establishments in the Midlands for nearly a quarter of a century before that. The father, Thomas Wright Hill, was an idealist, but he was quite incapable of dealing satisfactorily with business affairs, so poverty had forced him to employ his eldest sons, as instructors, from a very early age. Rowland, the third boy, was teaching from the age of eleven.

As he grew older, this Rowland started to display unusual qualities. He was ceaselessly ready to experiment—with his own diet, for instance. He lived for many periods of three days each on only two kinds of food, confining himself, during one of these spells of privation, to boiled green peas and salt, and, during another, to damson pie and sugar.

From his earliest youth, it was Rowland Hill's ambition to establish a school for the children of the upper and middle classes at which the science and practice of education might be improved 'to such a degree as to show that it is now in its infancy'. Before 1819, young Hill had been made Chief Director of the family establishment. In that year, he decided to move the school to a place called 'Hazelwood' where he built a new schoolhouse, acting as his own architect and his own clerk of works. At Hazelwood, he established a curious system of government—the school was to be run by the boys, he said, rather than by the teachers. Corporal punishment, in the new régime, was forbidden, and order was to be maintained by a 'court of justice' in which boys acting as magistrates, jury and constables would enforce more up-to-date penalties, such as compulsory sweeping of the playground. For guidance, he gave the pupils a constitution and a code of laws that filled more than a hundred closely printed pages. The system seems to have been quite successful, and discipline was kept up, but—said one of his ex-pupils, in later years—'this was done at too great a sacrifice. The thoughtlessness, the spring, the elation of childhood were taken from us; we were premature men.'

Soon, in spite of these reservations, the Hills' school became more widely known. Its reputation spread to all parts of the British Isles in 1822 when Rowland's elder brother Matthew published a book describing the family system, and it became famous all over the world two years later when Thomas De Quincey reviewed the book in the *London Magazine*. Immediately, boys started to pour in on the school in large numbers, from the newly founded republics of South America, from Greece, and from various other centres of enlightenment. To cope with this flood, the Hill family left Birmingham's provincial Hazelwood and moved closer to the metropolis—taking, as we have said, Tottenham's historic Bruce Castle.

A few years after the school was satisfactorily installed at Bruce Castle and running—for a nineteenth-century educational establishment—relatively sweetly, Rowland Hill, who had an extraordinary supply of energy and an endlessly inventive mind, started to lose interest in it. The postal system of England, or rather the lack of a proper postal system, began to engage his attention instead, and soon he was devoting nearly all his time to reforming the mail, being remembered, today, chiefly as the originator of the penny post. There is a permanent exhibition in Bruce Castle now of fascinating material connected with the post office, particularly during the period 1700–1840, and containing a number of items that relate directly to the years when the great postal innovator was still living in the house.

Little more than a stone's throw from the pleasant cedar-shaded park at the rear of Bruce Castle is the stadium at White Hart Lane which is, as every keen soccer fan knows, the headquarters of the famous Tottenham Hotspurs Football Club.

The 'Spurs', as they are universally known, started their activities on Tottenham Marshes in 1882, when the members of one of the local cricket clubs decided to set up some goal posts so that they could start playing a less leisurely game. The name of the club was derived from Harry Hotspur, the fiery fifteenth-century Earl of Northumberland whose deeds were celebrated by William Shakespeare in his play *Henry the Fourth, Part Two*. Hotspur was, of course, a forbear of Tottenham's own personal Duke, who could be reasonably expected to be a financially rewarding patron.

Tottenham Hotspurs won undying renown in 1901, when they became the first club to bring the Football Association's Cup to the South of England. (They defeated Sheffield United at Bolton, having drawn the first Final at the Crystal Palace.) They were victorious, again, in the Cup Final of 1921. They became Champions of Division Two of the English League in the 1949–50 season, and in the following year they won the championship of Division One, a feat accomplished only twice before in the whole history of professional football.

The streets around the White Hart Lane ground contain plenty of evidence of the local tradesmen's loyalty to their club. Near the Spurs Supporters' Club one can see 'The Spurs Shop', 'The Hotspur Motors', 'The Hotspur Grill and Steak House' and several similar signs. Plate glass windows are smashed occasionally when the football club's less responsible supporters express their loyalty with excessive zeal.

As the residential areas of Tottenham were developed, so, too, was the land right by the River Lea. This was especially suitable for industrial development, since the river had been for several centuries a very satisfactory working waterway. Of all the industrial undertakings to be seen, now, on the western bank of the Lea between Tottenham and the northern boundaries of Enfield, the neighbouring borough, the most interesting is, without much doubt, the oldest of them all—the Royal Small Arms Factory at Enfield Lock.

As long ago as 1653, the military experts of Cromwell's Long Parliament requested their Ordnance Officer to negotiate with John and Henry Wrath, of Enfield, 'for the use of certain mills in their possession on the River Lea, called *The Lock*, for making gunpowder'. Probably, the isolated nature of the site would make it especially suitable for such a dangerous purpose.

Then, when England went to war with France at the end of the eighteenth century, and it became apparent that this country could no longer rely on being able to obtain small arms from abroad, but would have to depend on its own resources, the members of the Board of Ordnance instructed a Major John By to establish and take charge of a small arms factory on the site of the old Gunpowder Mills by the Lea. By carried out his duties with great credit until 1821 when the establishments of the army were reduced and he was placed on the unemployed list. (He went to Canada after that, and founded a small village that he called 'Bytown'. This settlement became known later, as it grew, as 'Ottawa'.)

In its early years, the men in By's Enfield factory were mainly engaged in the assembly of the 'Brown Bess' muskets that were needed by the troops fighting Napoleon Buonaparte, over the Channel. Then, in 1816, the production of gun barrels was transferred from Lewisham to the Leaside works and the factory on the old Gunpowder Mills site grew perceptibly larger. Seven years after that, the factory won its first major contract when it was asked to produce five thousand Baker rifles, the Rifle Brigade being specially mustered to make use of them.

This may have seemed a very big deal. In those days, though, the workers in the Enfield factory depended on numerous subcontractors, each of whom made some separate part of the weapon, sending these components to Enfield to be assembled. During the Crimean War, *The Times* declared that the Enfield rifle 'smote the Russians like the hand of a destroying angel', but when the Government tried to increase the production of the factory, they ran into trouble. As the Inspector of Artillery at Woolwich told a committee of inquiry: 'The system hitherto adopted to procure small arms is so heterogeneous in character that it could not fail to produce considerable difficulties. The Government establishment at Enfield is comparatively small, and of a mixed nature, some parts of the work being performed by the Establishment, some by Contractors . . . The principal part of the gun trade upon which the Government mainly depends for supply in cases of emergency is carried on in Birmingham and London, and by men working by hand in wretched cellars and garrets, and great evil arises from the slowness of manufacture . . .'

In 1854, the members of the Board of Ordnance, needing to smite the Russians still harder, decided to take the entire manufacture of small arms into their own hands. To make this possible, they completely re-organised the Enfield factory, demolishing most of the existing buildings and putting up others in their place. Then, they purchased some very sophisticated machinery from the Ames Manufacturing Company of Massachusetts and Robbins and Lawrence of Connecticut, and with the new plant they made their Enfield factory famous for the extreme precision of its engineering.

The factory, today, is well worth studying as an extraordinarily fine example of Victorian industrial development. Much of the production work is still carried out in the main machine shop that was put up at the time of the Crimean War. The size and construction of this workshop—called, almost from the start, the 'Large Room'—greatly impressed the British queen and her subjects. The *Boys' Own Paper* of 1860 invited its readers to imagine: 'A single room more than an acre in extent, lofty, and well lit, in which some thousand men and boys are incessantly employed in superintending machinery. The ear is pained by the hum of fly-wheels, which revolve in thousands till the eye is giddy with their whirl. Miles of shafting are spinning round mistily, with a monotonous hum; the room is almost darkened, and the view completely obscured by some fifty or sixty thousand feet of broad, flapping lathe-bands, which are driving no less than six hundred machines, all going together with a tremulous rapidity and ease that seem to swallow up the work like magic . . .'

The iron columns that support the ridge-and-furrow roof of the Large Room are curiously embellished: cast on each column, at the 1854 rebuilding, were the initials of the Board of Ordnance—which, since that time, have gained unfortunate personal connotations—and a broad arrow of the kind used then to show that something or someone was the property, or in the custody, of the Government. (In the sixteenth century, Sir Philip Sidney, Master of the Ordnance, had chosen to mark the royal guns with a 'pheen' or heraldic broad arrow head, and this symbol of ownership had been employed for the same purpose ever since.)

Around the main production workshop, the members of Queen Victoria's Board of Ordnance put up a variety of other useful buildings—administrative offices, store houses, rolling mills, a foundry and engine house, a 'Mechanic's Institute' and library, an 'excessively pretty church' and a hotel for accommodating visitors to the factory—and many of these are still standing and in use today. There are rows of trim terrace houses, rushed up at the same time to accommodate the factory workers who were induced to move into the area, and in Ordnance Road, which runs in a westward direction from the factory, there are several 'commodious and desirable villas', standing in relatively spacious grounds, that were intended to house the factory's principal officers and their families. There are still a number of walnut trees growing in the immediate neighbourhood that were originally planted to provide wood for the stocks of the rifles produced in the factory. The Enfield works was a remarkably self-contained community in the 1860s and it has managed to retain a little of its exclusive atmosphere right down—or up—to the present day.

The Borough of Enfield, in which the Royal Small Arms Factory stands, includes the former boroughs of Enfield, Edmonton and Southgate. During the days of the Saxon, Norman, Plantagenet, Tudor and Stuart kings, the western and northern parts of the area were heavily wooded, and were kept almost exclusively for hunting. (From the time of King Henry IV, 'Enfield Chase' was one of the principal royal preserves. Southgate was, in fact, the 'south gate' of the Chase.)

In 1777, the ground at Enfield was 'dischased', or made available for other purposes but hunting. Roads were laid across it, and from that time on the land was developed for agricultural purposes with, in the south-eastern parts, a certain amount of building. The delightfully rural nature of the district, which is all the more surprising in view of its proximity to the closely packed streets of Wood Green and Tottenham, is still ensured by the continued existence of an unusually large number of beautifully treed parks, those at Forty Hill, Trent Park and White Webbs being especially extensive.

Even before the accession of Queen Victoria, the district seems to have been particularly favoured, for residential purposes, by comfortably-off persons whose occupations took them daily into the capital. Communication between Enfield and London was kept up by horse-drawn coaches which ran twice a day or even oftener, and those who walked to Edmonton could save half the fare by taking the stage from there. The most frequented coach was owned by a Mr. Glover, and it ran twice a day with six 'inside passengers' between Enfield and the Bank of England. Mr. Glover's enterprise started to fail soon after the railway came, offering the comforts of its swift, open trucks to potential commuters. The coach, taken off the roads, was purchased by a Mr. Waghorn, who intended to use it for the conveyance of mails between Alexandria and Suez. In 1849, a Mr. Bevan, a resident of Enfield Chase who happened to be staying in Alexandria, went for a walk one night after dinner and found 'Glover's Pride' lying abandoned in some squalid surroundings in, as Mr. Bevan put it, 'cobwebbed solitude'.

Enfield, today, still retains a little of the mellow atmosphere of a provincial market town, in spite of the efforts made by the civic authorities in recent years to 'improve' the place. Near St. Andrew's Church is the Grammar School, whose buildings include one, with a steep tiled roof and mullioned windows, that dates from the middle of the sixteenth century. From the quiet precincts of the old church, the ancient Holly Walk leads to Gentleman's Row, an intriguing cul-de-sac, with some superb Georgian houses that look out onto the carefully tended Chase Green Gardens.

Near Gentleman's Row flows the New River which was chiefly engineered by Sir Hugh Myddelton. Myddelton, who was a goldsmith and banker, served on the committee set up early in the seventeenth century to consider what could be done to relieve London's serious shortage of water. Having listened to a variety of wild and impracticable schemes, Myddelton offered to construct a conduit, himself, that would bring water from Amwell Springs, in Hertfordshire, through Enfield to Islington—a distance of thirty-eight miles. He began his excavations in 1609, and after encountering all kinds of difficulties, including opposition from landowners on the way, who feared that their property might be flooded, concluded his great enterprise on Michaelmas Day 1613, when his brother Sir Thomas Myddelton, who was Lord Mayor of London, officiated at the opening ceremony. In Enfield churchyard, still, there is a stone erected to the memory of John White, surveyor to the New River Company. The epitaph begins:

Here lies John White, who, day by day,
On river works did use much clay,
Is now himself turning that way

Both Edmonton and Enfield have interesting literary associations. It was to the Bell Inn at Edmonton, of course, that William

Cowper's 'citizen of credit and renown' John Gilpin, intended to travel:

> Tomorrow is our wedding-day, and we will then repair
> Unto the Bell at Edmonton, all in a chaise and pair

John Keats (1795–1821) spent much of his early life at his grandmother's home in Church Street, Edmonton, and studied at John Clarke's boarding-school at Enfield. Four years after Keats died, Charles Lamb visited Enfield with his poor sister Mary, who suffered from periodic fits of insanity, in one of which she had grabbed a knife and had killed their mother. The pair were so charmed by the district's rural beauties that Lamb, who had devoted himself to his sister's welfare, decided, in 1827, to settle locally. The house the Lambs rented can still be seen in Chase Side, and so too can the house next door (Number 89) into which the Lambs moved as lodgers when Mary's long attacks of mental sickness and depression made it no longer possible for her to keep house for her brother.

Most pathetic, perhaps, of all the dwellings associated with the Lambs is the little house in Church Street, Edmonton, to which Mary had to be taken in 1834 as a 'private mental patient'. At first, Lamb, who had become increasingly bored with the rustic inanities of Enfield, was delighted at the move, which took him 'three or four miles nearer the Great City'. His new-found happiness was not to last, however, for later in the same year he fell while out walking in Church Street and bruised his face so badly that erysipelas set in. On 27 December he died, and was buried in the churchyard just over the road from his last home. Mary survived him for thirteen years—having to be locked in a cupboard, which still exists, when she became more than usually violent—and, when she died, was buried beside him.

Another literary figure, though one who worked on a slightly more mundane level, perhaps, than Keats and Lamb, lived for many years in Silver Street, Enfield, at a handsome old weatherboarded house that is a little dwarfed, now, by the towering civic buildings that have been put up over the road. The man—Joseph Whitaker—was born in London in 1820 and was apprenticed at an early age to Mr. Barritt, a bookseller who had premises in Fleet Street. Whitaker was a man of much initiative who originated, successively, the *Penny Post*, the first monthly church magazine, the *Educational Register*, *Whitaker's Clergyman's Diary*, and, in January 1858, the *Bookseller*, which he intended primarily as a medium of information for publishers and retailers, but which was soon read eagerly by book-buyers generally as well. Whitaker's name became familiar wherever the English language was spoken when he brought out, in 1868, his *Almanack*, a compendium of useful information that is still re-issued annually and kept up-to-date today. It is an indication of Whitaker's skill that the form of the *Almanack*, like that of the *Bookseller*, has had to be changed only very slightly since it first appeared, other than to allow for natural expansion.

CHAPTER SIX

Waltham Abbey and Redbridge

IN the early Middle Ages, before the Lea was properly banked, the river was very difficult to cross—so difficult, that it became one of the principal lines of defence against the Danish invaders. To the east of the river, at that time, lay the Great Forest of Essex, which covered practically all the land now associated with that undulating county. Later, the shrinking but still extensive woodland became generally known as the 'Waltham Forest'—understandably, since the great Abbey of Waltham stood at one point on its boundaries. It was, wrote John Manwood, in his *Treatise of the Laws of the Forest*, published in 1665, 'a territory of woody ground and fruitful pastures, privileged for the wild beasts and the fowls of forest, chase and warren, to rest and abide there in the safe protection of the King, for his delight and pleasure'.

When those words were written the Forest of Waltham still covered many thousands of acres. It extended from Stratford on the west to Romford on the east, and the people who lived in the small villages of Walthamstow, Leyton and Chingford could all share in the resources and pleasures of their exceptional environment. As the population of London increased, though, the demand for corn grew too, and as the Lea Valley was conveniently close to the city, wide tracts of woodland and waste ground were cleared, enclosed, and ploughed, to become, in the process, the private property of landowners and wealthy farmers. The change was not always carried out with tact and discretion, however, and on several occasions the under-privileged cottagers protested against the loss of their traditional rights. At Leyton, in 1776, for instance, a Mr. Fowell applied to the local Vestry for permission to enclose a piece of ground in the neighbourhood. The members of the Vestry considered his application, and turned it down. Mr. Fowell, unimpressed, went ahead with his project. So, the Vestry passed a resolution that 'Davy the parish beadle do wait upon Mr. Fowell and acquaint him that unless he immediately pull down the wall by

1. Tillings' Horse Bus, taken outside Raynes Park Hotel, 1903

2a. Pinner High Street, 1908

2b. Grim's Dyke House, Harrow Weald. Drawn by R. Norman Shaw

3a. Column at Hadley, near Barnet, 1805. Engraving by Sands

3b. Early flying days at Hendon, 1912

4a. The First Sod. Mrs. S. A. Barnett lays the foundation of Hampstead Garden Suburb on 2 May, 1907

4b. Clarendon Cottage, Gentleman's Row, Enfield. It was occupied by Charles and Mary Lamb in 1825 and 1827

5a. View of Fairlop Oak in Epping Forest, 1802. Drawn and engraved by S. Rawle.

5b. The Clock Mill and House Mill at Stratford

6a. The Naval Asylum, Greenwich, 1811

6b. Crooms Hill

7a. John Flamsteed, First Astronomer Royal. Artist unknown

7b. A View of Greenwich, Deptford and London, taken from Flamsteed's Hill in Greenwich Park c. 1750

8a. Clapham Road, c. 1896

8b. Putney Bridge, 1904

him now building, the Vestry will proceed on Monday next to remove the encroachment'. Mr. Fowell eventually got his own way, but—as they say in East London today—'it cost him'. To appease the angry Vestrymen, he had to offer a hundred pounds for 'ye benefit of ye Poor of ye said Parish'. When less persuasive men than Mr. Fowell were concerned, such arguments tended to finish with blows.

In the year 1547, one of the forest villages, Walthamstow, was described in the *Register for Essex* as 'A great town having in it eighteen score housling people and more'. Nearly four hundred citizens, that is. Today, one can still walk round this historical village and from the remaining and well-preserved evidence one can still picture it as it was more than four hundred years ago.

The old village still has as its focal point, as it had then, the parish church that gives this most precious old world corner its most favoured name—'Church End'. The old church at Walthamstow is really old. It was built early in the twelfth century and it stands, almost certainly, on the site of a more ancient church still and probably one that had been a centre of worship there since Saxon times. There are about thirteen hundred visible monuments in and around the church, but the whole churchyard area is thought to have seen, during its long period of use, as many as twenty-six thousand human burials.

The timber-framed hall house near the church—it is usually called 'The Ancient House'—stands, it is believed, on the site of the original Manor House of Walthamstow. The present building is probably the one referred to, in his last will and testament, by Sir William Hyll, who was the Vicar of Walthamstow between the years 1470 and 1487. ('A tenement of mine called John Kykylwoldys', was Sir William's disposition, 'and ij acres in buryfield buttyng on the same tenement.') Originally, the building would have had a large open hall in the centre with, at one end, a raised room and, at the other, a 'solar'. By the middle of the eighteenth century, it had been divided into two separate tenements, an upper floor had been inserted, and dormer windows had been made in the central part of the roof to light the upper rooms. Mrs. Elizabeth Lucking, a widow, bought the house for £650 early in the nineteenth century. She held the property for forty years, during which time she further sub-divided it and 'developed' it so that it could be used as shops. In recent years it has been turned back into private dwellings again.

There are two notable sets of almshouses at Church End, Walthamstow. The older range stands on land acquired from the Prior and Vicar on Trinity Sunday, 16 June, 1527, so that the 'Right Worshipful Master George Monoux, Alderman of London' could build on it 'houses for pore folks and the edification and building for a Schole master and a ffree scole'. Much of the western end of the building was destroyed in an air raid on 8 October, 1940. The rebuilt part is a little higher than the rest, since modern legislation calls for refinements that would not have been dreamed of when Monoux's 'pore folks' were originally accommodated.

The second range of almshouses was founded in 1795 by a Mrs. Mary Squires who was a widow living at Newington. Mrs. Squires' almshouses were intended to provide homes for six widows of Walthamstow tradesmen, the widows to be fifty years of age and upwards. (They could be admitted at a younger age only if they suffered from weak eyesight or were lame.) The widows were to receive small annual stipends and each was to be given, on taking possession of her new home, a bedstead, a stove and a large water tub. In return for this generous treatment, the beneficiaries had to obey certain strict rules laid down by the foundress: they could not take in more than one 'nurse-child' apiece, they could undertake small washing and clear-starching but not heavy washing, and they were strictly forbidden to hang out any article in front of their quarters.

The Vestry House, situated at the junction of Vestry Road and Church Path, was built early in the eighteenth century to provide a meeting-place for the members of the local Vestry (the equivalent, almost of a modern town council, it was composed of 'all ratepayers in Vestry assembled'.) The building had also to provide accommodation for the twenty or thirty paupers who were likely to be a charge on the parish at any given time, and for the Workhouse Master who was appointed to rule them. (A tablet over the entrance has engraved on it this ominous message: 'If any would not work neither Should he eat'.) After the paupers were moved away to Stratford in 1840 the building, with its extension that had been put up in 1756, was used for thirty years to house the Walthamstow police and after they moved out it became the armoury for the local Volunteers. It is now a well-arranged museum of local history, its most notable exhibit being the 'Bremer Car', built between the years 1892 and 1895 by a Mr. Frederick Bremer of Walthamstow. This may well have been the first British car to have been driven by an internal combustion engine.

Unlike the Vestry House, which has been put to these varied uses since it was first added to the Walthamstow scene, the Infant School nearby has had a comparatively settled existence.

The school was brought into being at the beginning of the nineteenth century when Samuel Wilderspin, author of a book called *Early Discipline Illustrated*, tried to persuade the Reverend William Wilson, who was at that time the Vicar of Walthamstow, that such a school, run on the most up-to-date lines, was a practical proposition. At first, the good Vicar doubted, 'as the houses were widely scattered', if a sufficient number of children could be collected. He agreed to lend Wilderspin a barn that belonged to him, though, and when Wilderspin was proved right the good clergyman arranged to give the school a more suitable permanent home in a corner of his glebe. There, in the beautifully proportioned building that still stands, the district's 'infants'—aged, two to seven—were introduced to the art of arithmetic by graduated exercises which included 'Clapping the hands in measured time, in imitation of the masters . . . Learning by ear from a monitor on the rostrum the more simple combinations of number, addition, subtraction, multiplication, division and fractions . . . Examinations in the combinations of number . . . Mutual examination in the combination of number, the tables, and mental arithmetic, and Practice of arithmetic on slates . . .' Young people are still taught in the Reverend Wilson's building today, though not all the basic principles of Wilderspin's 'practicable and sufficient system of education' are followed as rigidly, perhaps, as they were during the first years of the reign of Queen Victoria.

Back in the days before Walthamstow became submerged, like the neighbouring villages of Leyton and Tottenham, in urban sprawl, a young lad named William Morris used to live at Water House on the outskirts of the town. From there, and from Woodford Hall, to which his parents moved when he was eight years old, the lad would set out to roam for hours through the surrounding countryside. 'What with the beasts and the men, and the scattered red-tiled roofs, and the big hayricks', he was to write nostalgically, 'it does not make a bad holiday to get a quiet pony and ride about there on a sunny afternoon of Autumn, and look over the river and the craft passing up and down, and on to Shooter's Hill and the Kentish uplands, and then turn round to the wide green sea of the Essex marshland, with the great domed line of the sky, and the sun shining down in one flood of peaceful light . . . To this day when I smell a May-tree, I think of going to bed by daylight.'

On these youthful journeys, Morris became imbued with the passionate love of flowers which he was never to lose, and which was to inspire him so consistently in his later life when, as England's greatest designer of fabrics, wallpapers and other decorative materials he was to have so profound an effect on the nation's taste. Water House, now standing in the carefully laid out grounds of Lloyd Park, contains today a small but effective Morris Museum.

Chingford, just over two miles to the north of Walthamstow and on slightly higher ground, is an airy, well-treed suburb that has developed from the ancient parish of the same name. In 1848, Chingford was described as 'an irregularly built but pleasing rural village'. Living and working there at that time were thirteen farmers, two wheelwrights, three blacksmiths, three shoemakers, a saddler, a harness maker, a builder, two grocers and a tailor. The population of the village at that time was less than a thousand. Only eight thousand, one hundred and eighty-four people were living there in 1911, many of them owning fine houses with large, well-tended gardens. The explosive increase in population that has made Chingford what it is today did not start until after the First World War.

There are two parish churches at Chingford, an old church, and a 'new' one. They were both built by The Ridgeway, an ancient road that runs along the spine of the high ground overlooking the Lea Valley.

The old parish church, dedicated to All Saints, was used from Norman times until the middle of the nineteenth century. By that time, the building had fallen into such a state of decay that it was no longer thought to be safe. So, it was abandoned, and a new church dedicated to St. Peter and St. Paul was built on Chingford Green, about a mile away. As the old church became, gradually, a ruin overgrown with creepers and ivy, its picturesque qualities made it a magnet to artists. It features, notably, in the background of Arthur Hughes' *Home from Sea*, the Pre-Raphaelite tear-jerker in which a young sailor lad is seen lying, apparently in some distress, among the ancient, mossy graves. In 1928, the church was completely renovated and restored at the expense of a Miss Boothby-Heathcote, daughter of the Rector who had had the new Chingford church built to the designs of Lewis Vulliamy. It is now a useful Parish Centre and meeting-place.

There are several interesting buildings to be admired, or wondered at, around the Green, besides Vulliamy's church with its fine spire and its unusual chequerboard enrichments. There are the Bull and Crown, a fine late Victorian public house, and, a little to the west of the church, the older King's Head, which has the remains of a splendid stable block. Behind this pub rises Pole Hill with, on its summit, an obelisk put up in 1824 by the Reverend John Pound, who was then the Astronomer Royal. Pound intended that this obelisk, when viewed from Greenwich Observatory, should mark true north. Unfortunately for his plans, the meridian was adjusted in 1884 and the true north line now lies nineteen feet to the east of the imposing but redundant pillar.

A little to the north of Pole Hill lie the borders of Epping Forest, a cherished remnant of the ancient Forest of Essex that has survived between the valleys of the Lea and the Roding and which covers, in all, an area of some nine square miles. There is little doubt that the Forest, which during the eighteenth and early nineteenth centuries was being rapidly made smaller by a variety of encroachments and enclosures, would have disappeared altogether by now had not the Corporation of the City of London decided to intervene. So, at the Corporation's instance, a Board of Commissioners was appointed, under the Epping Forest Act of 1871, and under the Board's guidance the Corporation managed to acquire the freehold interest of all the 5,600 acres of forest that remained, at that time, unenclosed. In 1882 the tract was declared open for the use of the public 'for ever', the ancient Court of Verderers being revived to exercise a kindly guardianship over this beautifully timbered land.

On the fringe of the Forest today, near the pleasant lake called 'Connaught Water', one can still see and visit the remarkable structure known as 'Queen Elizabeth's Hunting Lodge'. This building was put up in the sixteenth century so that royal visitors to the Chase and their guests might shoot from its galleries at deer driven in front of them by hounds. The lodge has been well maintained during the four and a half centuries that it has been in existence and it has been fitted up, today, as a museum of local history. Quite near the lodge is the East Essex Golf Club, whose members wear red shirts when they are playing, which all adds to the pastoral charm of this strange, outlying district of London.

The London Borough of Redbridge gets its name from the old 'Red Bridge' which used to span the River Roding where the Eastern Avenue now crosses the river by means of a wider and more modern piece of engineering. The borough contains within its boundaries three ancient villages—Woodford, Wanstead and Ilford—that were once set quite deeply in the forests of Epping and Hainault and must have witnessed in their time the arrival and departure of innumerable royal hunting parties. The villages started to grow and to become towns as late in time as the third quarter of the nineteenth century. Even before the outbreak of the First World War they seemed to have 'jelled', and since 1914 they have seen little change except for the construction of a few new housing estates, and the re-shaping of the centre of Ilford.

Woodford, at the north-west corner of the borough, might have emerged from rustic obscurity considerably earlier if the wells found there in the eighteenth century had really had some medicinal qualities, as was claimed. (The little 'spa' perished of neglect almost as soon as it was advertised.) The place got some more lasting publicity during the present century when its people, with those of nearby Wanstead, were represented in parliament for forty years by Mr. (later, Sir) Winston Churchill. To commemorate this notable connection, a statue of Sir Winston, executed by David McFall, R.A., and cast in bronze has been put up on Woodford Green. The figure, eight and a half feet high, was unveiled on the last day of October, 1959, by Field Marshal Viscount Montgomery, in the presence of Sir Winston and Lady Churchill.

Wanstead was famous once, for having as its principal feature a large mansion built in 1715 and the following years for Sir Richard Child. It was designed for him in the new 'Palladian' style by the great architect Colin Campbell. The grounds around the house were as splendid as the noble dwelling they were intended to enhance, having avenues of trees, an ornamental canal, and a decorative summer-house that survives—like one of the stable blocks, and the massive stone pillars that carried the main gates—to this day. The house, itself, has vanished, its fate being sealed when it was inherited at the end of the eighteenth century by a child named Catherine Tylney Long, who, having come into an income of £80,000 per year was one of the richest persons in England.

The rub came when Catherine grew up, and, wearing a wedding dress that cost seven hundred guineas, married a worthless young rake named William Pole Wellesley. Within ten years, Wellesley had got through practically all his wife's immense fortune (chiefly by gambling) and as a result the house and its contents had to be sold in an auction that lasted for thirty-two days. Less than two years after the house was demolished—it changed hands merely as building materials—the heart-broken lady was dead, and her three children had been made Wards in Chancery. Pole Wellesley married again, but his wife was no better than the first at keeping him in the luxury to which he thought he was entitled, and she ended her days in the workhouse.

In the autumn of 1921, an incident took place in one of the quiet residential streets of Ilford that was to earn the suburb some world-wide notoriety. Shortly before midnight on 3 October, an unhappily married couple named Mr. and Mrs. Thompson were returning to their home at No. 41 Kensington Gardens when they were approached in Belgrave Road by a nineteen-year-old shipping clerk called Frederick Bywaters who had been, for some time past, Mrs. Thompson's secret lover. The three people spoke together, and then there was a brief quarrel, at the climax of which Fred Bywaters drew a knife and plunged the point of it into his mistress' husband. Edith Thompson, crying hysterically, rushed off to summon assistance. When she returned with a doctor, Percy Thompson was dead.

After he was arrested, Bywaters made some determined efforts to shield Mrs. Thompson by taking all the blame himself. (This was his account of the tragic mix-up: 'I said to him: "You have got to separate from your wife." He said: "No." I said: "You will have to." We struggled. I took my knife from my pocket and we fought and he got the worst of it. Mrs. Thompson must have been spellbound, for I saw nothing of her during the fight.')

In spite of the young man's insistence on his mistress' innocence, both the surviving members of the ill-fated triangle were charged with murder. Indiscreet letters that Mrs. Thompson had written to Bywaters were found by the police and seemed in the eyes of the law to prove her complicity beyond any doubt. Even so, Mrs. Thompson might well have been acquitted if she had not been a little too fond of striking dramatic attitudes. Seeing herself in the rôle of a great tragic figure who could not fail to sway twelve good men and true by the pathetic appeal of a personal appearance, she spurned the wise advice of her counsel Sir Henry Curtis-Bennett, who asked her not to give evidence, and she insisted on going into the witness box.

Her obstinacy proved fatal. Under the ruthless cross-examination of the Solicitor General, Sir Thomas Inskip, Mrs. Thompson's self-confidence dwindled, and she failed to persuade the members of the jury that she had not known in advance of Bywaters' intentions, as she had felt sure that she would be able to do. So, in spite of some inspired advocacy by her counsel, both she and Bywaters were found guilty of murder and sentenced to death. Their appeals, heard by the Lord Chief Justice of England, were unsuccessful. ('The case was clearly put before the jury', said the Lord Chief Justice. 'There was ample evidence, partly direct evidence, partly evidence from which inference might properly be drawn; and upon that evidence, in a case which exhibits from beginning to end no redeeming feature . . . this appeal must be dismissed.') A petition organised on Mrs. Thompson's behalf was signed by many thousands of people, but that too failed to save her life. The judicial execution of the Ilford housewife by hanging on the dark morning of 9 January, 1923 is said to have been one of the most sordid events in British penal history. Before long, the man who had the horrible job of despatching Mrs. Thompson had, himself, committed suicide.

The north-east corner of the Borough of Redbridge contains the extensive tract of ground that was known, once, as the 'Hainault Forest'. It was part, previously, of the very much larger Forest of Essex. The most famous tree in this part of the forest for at least two centuries was known as the 'Fairlop Oak'. This monster is believed to have had a trunk sixty-six feet in circumference, from which seventeen huge branches issued, most of them measuring not less than twelve feet in girth.

Early in the eighteenth century, a benevolent pump and block maker named Daniel Day, of Wapping, decided to take his work-people on an annual outing. They would go to the Forest, he decreed, and they would make the Fairlop Oak their rendezvous. At 7.30 a.m. on the first Friday of each July after that, a strange procession would set out from Wapping. The chief guests travelled in a waterman's boat, the *Unity*, which was mounted on wheels and drawn by six gaily decorated horses. A band and outriders were in attendance, and the gaudy throng caused considerable commotion as it set out for the country. At Mile End Road, the procession would be joined by the block makers, with their boat *The Maggot*, which was also drawn by six horses. Under the widely spreading boughs of the Fairlop Oak, when they reached it, Mr. Day and his jovial companions would consume a lavish banquet of pork and beans, the menu for the feast being exactly the same each year. Round the Oak were arranged booths, shies, and other amenities of a traditional fairground.

By the middle of the eighteenth century, the annual excursion to Fairlop had become one of London's most popular entertainments, as many as a hundred thousand people being drawn through Ilford and Fairlop to the fair in the forest. The Governors of the Forest heartily disapproved of this noisy annual invasion of their territories, and in 1765 the members of the Forest Court instructed their keepers to discourage the fair. The keepers did their best, but the function was much too popular to be easily suppressed, and it was still being held in 1820 when the ancient oak, by that time very much decayed, was finally blown down.

Not even the loss of the famous old tree could stop the annual beano, though (in 1839, missionaries from the Religious Tract Society counted, disapprovingly, 72 gaming tables and 108 places for drinking at the fair in the forest) and the merrymakers continued to wend their way, once every year, in an armada of carriages, landaus, barouches and other vehicles to the spot where it had stood. This went on until 1851, when the people who lived in the neighbourhood complained so bitterly about the depredations caused by the local deer that the trees which had surrounded the great oak were all felled and the adjoining parts of the forest were converted into farmland. The 'forest fair' went on being held even after that—as late as 1892, the procession was still being organised—but by that time the Bald Hind Inn at Chigwell had become the centre of the festivities.

The name 'Fairlop', today, is principally applied to an area of nearly one thousand acres of charmingly rural countryside crossed by only three roads, the Forest Road, Hainault Road and Painters Road. It is still being mainly used, as this book is being prepared, as farmland. To have nearly one thousand acres of fair agricultural land in such a heavily populated suburban area might have been considered an advantage, but this is not so. Predictably, says a recent Borough Council handout, Fairlop will change. It has been seen, in a Greater London Development Plan, as an 'Area of Opportunity', a designation which has ominous undertones. If all goes according to the planners' intentions, this sweet and unspoiled fragment of the Green Belt will become a 'drive-in, leisure-packed, recreational centre' which will cater for all tastes and interests. Space will be allocated for 'noisy pursuits involving powered vehicles', and a lively atmosphere will be created 'in the vicinity of a visually exciting sportsdrome or athletics stadium'. The area will be so busy, say the planners, that it may need its own transport system to enable people to get from one part to another. Alas, poor Fairlop!

CHAPTER SEVEN

From the Tower to Barking

THE suburbs of London that lie just to the north of the Thames, and downstream from The Tower, have long been renowned for three things—for crime of various kinds, for dirt, and for anarchy. They are being cleaned up quite effectively today, but there are still some pretty squalid corners to be seen in the Boroughs of Tower Hamlets, Newham and Barking.

These districts have been directly connected with the City of London for many centuries by the great Roman road which crossed the River Lea at the Old Ford. After the ford, the road passed on through the Leyton marshes to Stratford and on, from there, to Ilford, Romford and Chelmsford. (Eventually, the legionaries would reach Colchester, where the Romans had a camp.) The road must have been an important one even as early as A.D. 693, for it was featured in the news in that year when Erkenwald, Bishop of London, died at Barking while he was on a visit to his sister Ethelburga, who was the first abbess of the important convent at that town. The convent was destroyed by the Danes in 870 and restored later, by King Edgar.

Another important religious house and seat of learning was founded at West Ham in 1135 by William de Montfichet, who was the district's manorial lord. This monastery, the Abbey of Stratford Langthorne, stood on the east bank of the Channelsea, which is one of the principal tributaries of the River Lea. In its time, the Stratford Abbey was one of the wealthiest and most influential of all the hundred-odd houses held by the Cistercian Order in England. All its buildings have vanished now, though, and the only traces that remain of it are two stone window arches set in the long porch of West Ham parish church, a carved stone in the church's tower, and a font bowl. After the abbey was dissolved by Henry VIII, the district was left in dire poverty, the rogues and vagabonds taken on the great highway being a constant drain on the resources of the parish.

From Norman times at least there have been mills or groups of mills on the River Lea and its tributaries at West Ham. (Some, in this area, were recorded in the Domesday Book, and others on the site were owned, until the Dissolution, by the Abbey of Stratford Langthorne.) Two mills only have survived to the present day—the Clock Mill, dated 1817, with its polygonal clock tower that is more than half a century older, and the handsome House Mill, built in 1776, with its steeply pitched Welsh slate roof, which has much of its original machinery still intact. Approached by a delightful nineteenth-century road paved with stone setts and flagstones, this small group of industrial buildings is one of the most splendid architectural features in the whole of the heavily industrialised Lea Valley.

The move towards this industrialisation began during the seventeenth century, when a few other small undertakings were started in the vicinity of the Lea mills. These undertakings seem to have aroused much of the same kind of resentment that similar establishments have a tendency to cause today. In 1614, according to the local court records: 'The jury present Lancelot Gamblyn lately of Stratford Langthorne, starchmaker, because by his unlawful making of starch such a stink and ill-favour continue and daily arise so that the liege subjects of the present King along the highway in Stratford Langthorne are not able to come and go as accustomed without great danger to their lives through the loathsome smell . . .'

In 1676 William Sherwin, thought to be the first English calico printer, took out a patent and established a works by the River Lea where he could rely on a plentiful supply of pure water, combined with wide expanses of open ground, near the river, where his cloths could bleach and dry. By the middle of the eighteenth century there were eighty acres of 'calico grounds' by the Channelsea. Even as late as 1851, when a census was taken, there were as many as 250 people in the district who were still engaged in the silk and calico printing and allied trades.

During the eighteenth century, the calico printers were joined by the porcelain manufacturers. In 1744, Thomas Frye, a painter and engraver of West Ham, and Edward Heylyn, a glass blower of Bow, took out the first patent for the manufacture, in England, of this attractive and translucent material. For about four years, the two men experimented at Heylyn's premises at Bow. Then, in

1748, Frye took out a further patent and, backed financially by Alderman Arnold of the City of London he set up a works on the north side of the Stratford High Street, between Bow Bridge and the present Marshgate Lane.

Frye's factory was constructed, as far as possible, on the lines of one at Canton, in China. The whole building was heated by two huge stoves that were built against the outside walls. From these stoves, the heat needed for the various processes was carried to the remoter parts of the premises through a complicated system of pipes and flues. In its heyday, the Bow works provided a reasonable living for as many as three hundred people, but working in the oven-like factory must have been almost unbearably uncomfortable. Frye is said to have ruined his own health by spending too many hours, continuously, in its torrid interior, so that he was forced to retire in 1759. The works continued—producing some exquisite porcelain—until business troubles forced the proprietors to close down in 1776.

While West Ham, East Ham and Barking were indeed isolated hamlets, surrounded by unspoiled country, in the seventeenth and eighteenth centuries, many of their residents made handsome livings in the smuggling trade. Usually, the contraband material would be landed at some convenient spot in the riverside marshes for there were plenty of little creeks and gulleys where such activities could pass almost unnoticed. From there, the smuggled goods would be carried inland in carts or wagons that had been specially adapted for the purpose, the space under a false floor usually being used for concealing the precious freight. On one occasion, it is known, the excise officers hunted with such determination for a load of smuggled brandy that the kegs of spirit had to be hidden in the rushes close to the Thames. Somehow, the news of the smugglers' evasive action leaked out, and on the following day thirty or forty of the inhabitants of East Ham and West Ham went down to the river armed with a variety of cans and other drinking utensils. After a brief hunt, they managed to find and uncover the carefully concealed kegs. Within a very short time they had become so helplessly inebriated that most of them were quite incapable of finding their own way home.

'Body snatching', too, was practised very profitably by a gang who concentrated principally on the burying grounds of East Ham, Barking and Ilford. The good people of East Ham first became aware that bodies were being snatched in their district shortly after one of the village women died of a malignant growth. On the Sunday after the funeral, her husband and her children went to visit her grave. As they approached it, the children picked up a number of ribbons which, they knew, had been enclosed with their mother's body in her coffin. On examining the grave, the members of the bereaved family found that it had been opened, and that the body that it had contained had been taken away. When anyone was buried at East Ham after that, the grave was guarded carefully for at least a fortnight. Beyond two weeks, it was thought, a grave was not likely to be disturbed.

In 1827, a certain Mrs. Kingshott died in East Ham. The doctors were anxious to hold an autopsy to establish the cause of her death, but the husband would not hear of it, so the lady was buried. The next day, a Mr. Adams happened to be passing Morley's Corner when three men stopped him and asked a number of questions. Adams guessed, from the nature of their inquiries, what they were after; so, he went to Mr. Kingshott's friends and advised them to put on extra watchers. They took the hint and, instead of posting three men to keep watch on the grave they instructed eight men to hide in the church porch and await events.

The eight men had not been there long before the three strangers appeared, went to Mrs. Kingshott's grave, and started to dig. Out from the church porch rushed the watchers, in time to grab two of the men. The third man, attempting to hide, climbed into a wagon which was standing nearby. The wagon was loaded with manure, however, and before the man could extricate himself and get away again he was apprehended. All three men were then taken to the horse pond by the White Horse tavern, ropes were tied round their bodies, and they were dragged repeatedly through the water. They would have been lynched after that—hung up from the sign post of the White Horse, it was intended—had they not been saved by the intervention of one of the local landowners who persuaded the angry villagers to take the frightened men to Barking Gaol. In spite of the fact that these men were sentenced to terms of imprisonment, body-snatching continued in the district for some little time.

Long before boxing became a more or less respectable sport, the best prize fights staged in the whole of the London area took place, often, in the woods and marshes round East Ham. Before one of these bloody protracted and entirely illegal battles, as many as sixty or seventy 'flies' or 'chariots' might be seen approaching the unpoliced village from the direction of London. (The old, comparatively straight road that led from the metropolis to the eastern counties was comparatively well-surfaced, and was, therefore, doubly well-suited—it could be watched, for the distant approach of The Law and quick get-aways could be made on it, to east or west.) The ring would be pitched at a little distance from the public road, and large sums of money would be staked on the outcome of the contest. The last of these clandestine fights took place, it is believed, at the end of November, 1839. By the time the loser had been battered into subjection, a dense fog had descended on the district, and the spectators were quite unable to find their way back to the London road. There were two or three very deep ponds, at the time, between the White Horse tavern and the church. Nine of the stylish conveyances that had come down from London were driven, in the resulting confusion, into these ponds, and the local farm hands earned some welcome sovereigns by helping to drag them out.

From the accounts of smuggling, corpse stealing and illicit pugilism given in the last few pages, it might seem that West Ham and East Ham, during the eighteenth and nineteenth centuries, lacked citizens with any high moral purpose in their lives, but this was far from being the case, for there was, in fact, a small colony of reasonably wealthy Quakers who had bought or built houses in and around Upton Lane. In 1762, for instance, Doctor John Fothergill, the well-known Quaker botanist, purchased one of the local estates and developed it into a botanical garden that was reckoned, by the time it was at its best, to be second only to the garden at Kew.

Then, Samuel Gurney the Quaker banker and philanthropist came to live at Ham House and made it a meeting-place for many of those who were pressing for the abolition of the slave trade, and other reforms. In 1800, Gurney's sister Elizabeth married Joseph Fry, son of the owner of nearby Plashet House. Thirteen years later, Mrs. Fry decided to do something positive about the appalling conditions in Newgate Prison, where three hundred women and children were confined in two grossly overcrowded bug-ridden wards and two wholly inadequate cells, without any warmth, without any bed clothes, and with no facilities for washing themselves. Visiting the unfortunate prisoners as often as she could, Mrs. Fry tried to comfort and cheer them while, in political circles, she agitated for steps to be taken that would lead, as rapidly as possible, to prison reform. Her campaign, in the course of which she travelled to all parts of the country, was carried on in its later stages from the house in the Portway to which she moved in 1829. Joseph Jackson Lister, another Quaker, lived across Upton Lane at Upton House and his son Joseph Lister (later, Lord Lister) the pioneer of antiseptic surgery was born there in 1827.

Between 1851 and 1881 the population of West Ham increased enormously—from 18,817 to 128,953 in fact—the growth of the town being, in the words of the West Ham Local Board, 'unprecedented in the annals of parochial history in this country'. The district lay just outside the area covered by the Metropolis Buildings Act of 1844, which, with the Slaughterhouse Act of 1874, placed heavy restrictions on those who wanted to carry on 'offensive' trades within the boundaries of the capital. So, bone boilers and leather tanners and the manufacturers of such smelly or potentially smelly substances as chemical manure, ink, soap, naphtha, varnish and vitriol flocked to the banks of the Lea and of the Thames near where the Lea flowed into it. There, land was still relatively cheap, and—this was an important point—could still be bought to be held, freehold, right to the water's edge. Many of the workers who live in West Ham today earn their wages or salaries in trades that cannot be truthfully described as pleasant.

The suburbs on the north bank of the Thames were built, largely, as Britain's overseas trade developed. Their history can hardly be separated, therefore, from the history of London's dockland. By 1660, there was a very real need for proper docks to be built in the London area. By law, at that time, all the goods that were brought up the Thames to the City had to be landed at one of the officially authorised quays situated between London Bridge and the Tower of London, and those quays just could not accommodate even a small percentage of the vessels that were brought into the rapidly burgeoning port.

The first reasonably commodious dock to be made by the Thames was constructed around the year 1660 by the members of the East India Company, who needed such a facility for fitting out their large and handsome ships before they sent them off to the remotest known corners of the globe. The members of the company decided to build their dock on the Isle of Dogs—the low-lying horseshoe-shaped peninsula, opposite Greenwich, round which, since medieval times, high walls had had to be built to prevent inundations from the river's merciless tides. These walls—the Mill Wall on the west, on which at one time as many as seven windmills turned, and the 'Bleak' or Black Wall on the east—have given their names, respectively, to one of East London's grimmer suburbs and to the under-river tunnel which, in the twentieth century, serves thousands of East London's daily commuters.

As well as the East India Company's dock, a number of 'sufferance wharves' with limited privileges were constructed to provide additional accommodation for the river's shipping. These, in their turn, soon proved insufficient, and by the third quarter of the eighteenth century as many as two thousand vessels might be jostling for elbow room, at any one time, in the foully polluted waters of London's Upper Pool. The thieving carried on in this cramped and slummy reach by 'River Pirates, Night Plunderers, Light Horsemen, Heavy Horsemen, Scuffle Hunters, and Mudlarks' made trading with London merchants a risky if not positively unprofitable business. (Towards the end of the century, no fewer than 559 refineries in the London area were said to be operating on raw sugar stolen from ships on the river.)

So, in 1799, a Bill was passed by Parliament authorising the construction of a new 'West India' dock in the low-lying ground between Limehouse Reach and Blackwall Reach. (Actually, two docks were built, with a fine range of warehouses nearby that could be guarded by a posse of armed men.) The new docks were officially opened, with much pomp, by the Prime Minister, Henry Addington, on 22 August, 1802 and proved so successful that further docks were then made—the London Dock (opened in 1805), the East India Docks (1806), St. Katherine's Dock (1828), the Victoria Dock (1850), the Milwall Dock (1868) and the Albert Dock (1880) being the most important. As the docks spread gradually up and down Thames-side, a number of little country hamlets, Blackwall, Limehouse, Ratcliff, Shadwell and Wapping among them, almost completely lost their identities as huge numbers of cheap houses were put up around them. In the new, mean terraces, thousands of people lived, slept, worked and died in the service of the great riverside industries.

If one had walked through dockland during the 1850s when the historian Henry Mayhew made his survey of *London Labour and the London Poor*, one would have seen men with sweaty faces dyed permanently blue from handling cargoes of indigo, and 'coal whippers' black with dust from the roots of their hair to the tips of their finger nails. As one coal-whipper told Mayhew: 'I have known the coal dust to be that thick in a ship's hold that I've been unable to see my mate, though he was only two feet from me.'

In spite of the appalling conditions in which they had to labour, there was no shortage of applicants for employment in the docks. Only a comparatively few, relatively fortunate workers were on the lists to be regularly employed. Thousands of other men congregated at the dockheads every morning. These were 'casual workers', mostly penniless Irish countrymen who had newly arrived in London, or totally unskilled refugees from half the countries of Europe. Then, recorded Mayhew, the foreman would read out names from a book while those whose names were not called 'jumped on the backs of others . . . all shouting . . . thousands of men struggling for one day's hire, the scuffle being made the fiercer by the knowledge that hundreds out of the numbers there assembled must be left to idle the day out in want'. Now, many of the dark riverside alleys where the men fought like animals for employment are being refashioned. Docks are being closed and drained, and many of the vast echoing warehouses are being demolished, or are being converted into expensive and highly desirable 'executive' dwellings.

In a community that developed as rapidly as the one bounded by the great Romford Road to the north and the River Thames to the south, there was a real need for good places of entertainment. For several centuries, there had been notable theatres in East London. They had been built there because Puritan restrictions had made it almost impossible, from the sixteenth century onwards, for anyone to put up a permanent public playhouse inside the City boundaries. As the Lord Mayor and Aldermen had observed in a letter they sent to the Privy Council on 28 July, 1597: '[Theatres] are the ordinary places for vagrant persons, masterless men, thieves, horse-stealers, whoremongers, cozeners, coney-catchers, contrivers of treason and other idle and dangerous people . . . [They] maintain idleness in such persons as have no vocation, and draw apprentices and other servants from their ordinary works and all sorts of people from . . . sermons and other Christian exercises to the great hindrance of trades and profanation of religion . . .'

With such sentiments around, the provision of extra-mural playhouses became almost inevitable. But, these playhouses were to be found, principally in Bethnal Green, Hackney, Hoxton, Stepney and other centres of population that could be easily reached by those living in the capital. They were much too far from East Ham, West Ham and Barking to attract any nineteenth-century bone boilers or leather tanners who might require a little healthy entertainment, with their ladies, after a hard day's work.

At first, the demand for theatres in the newly populated districts was partly satisfied by companies of strolling players, who performed in tents like circuses do today, or in any building that they could hire temporarily and in which they could possibly erect a stage and seat an audience.

Then, in 1884, an actor manager called Charles Silver, alias Dillon, applied to the Stratford magistrates for a licence that would allow him to build and open a permanent theatre in the area. The proposal met with the approval of the local press—the *Stratford Express* pointed out that there was no provincial town of the size of Stratford without its theatre—but it was opposed by the Vicar of St. John's Church, Stratford, who, 'on behalf of all the clergy, Nonconformist ministers, Catholic priests, various employers of labour and local school teachers' presented a petition to the Bench against the grant of a licence, claiming that the establishment of a theatre would not be good for the moral elevation of the neighbourhood. The very position of the proposed theatre would necessitate a very low kind of drama, pleaded the Vicar. The place would become the resort of the district's lowest characters. It would be much too near the Respectable Home for Young Women, which, said the Vicar, had recently been erected by certain philanthropic ladies in the immediate vicinity.

In spite of the Vicar's protests, the Bench granted Dillon the licence he asked for because, as the Chairman pointed out, it was easier to keep control over a licensed permanent theatre than over a part-time movable fit-up.

The new theatre—converted, in the main, from an existing wheelwright's workshop and called, like so many playhouses opened at the time, the 'Theatre Royal'—was judged by the local press 'pretty and attractive' inside, though the exterior was decried as 'ugly'. In a determined effort to appeal to the better instincts of his audiences and in a vain resolve, as the *Stratford Express* put it 'to make the theatre a home for the drama as distinguished from the dreary pieces in which the uninstructed delight to witness a murder every twenty minutes', Dillon offered in his opening week Lord Lytton's uplifting tragedy *Richelieu*, and, in the following week, an equally inspiring piece entitled *Belphegor*. His choice of plays was approved by the 'dramatic critic' sent round by the local *Express*, but the less wealthy Stratford citizens packed tightly together in the gallery were not so readily impressed, for they cracked nuts and chewed the kernels noisily through almost the whole of each performance. At last, Dillon found that he could stand this irreverent behaviour no longer. Angrily, he strode out in front of the curtain and gave the masticators in his gallery a thorough dressing-down. 'You treat me fairly and I will treat you fairly, and will give you good entertainment', he concluded. 'But I certainly will not have the beautiful lines of this play spoiled and my artistes insulted by your rude behaviour.' Dillon's speech was greeted with resounding applause from the more select quarters of the house.

From 1884 until 1957, the Theatre Royal at Stratford belonged to one member or other of the famous Fredericks family, to whom Dillon was directly related. During that time the fortunes of the house alternately flourished and declined, according to the efficiency, or otherwise, of its various managers and tenants, and the attractions of the fare offered to the East London citizens. 'Poole's Grand Dioramic Excursions'—forerunners of the moving pictures—drew large audiences to the theatre in July 1887. By 1909, the patrons were paying hard-earned pence to see plays with a 'high moral tone'. The nature of these improving entertainments is indicated by this selection from their titles: *A Girl's Temptation*, *The Branded Woman*, *The Girl who Went Astray*, *Dark Deeds of the Night* and *No Mother to Guide Her*. Melodramas with lurid titles such as *The Painted Woman*, *Shall We Forgive Her*? and *A Mother Should Tell*—tenth rate playlets that had been out of date since before the First World War—were still being staged at the Theatre Royal in the early 1930s. Few people went to see them. With the cinema, then, providing a powerful alternative attraction, the days of the 'legitimate' stage in East London seemed to be numbered.

In a despairing attempt to keep the live theatre alive, an ex-

Naval Petty Officer named John Williams took the 'Royal' in 1935 and presented his wife, Ivy Maurice, in a succession of dramas and melodramas, offering as many as four different plays every week. In addition to such famous old stormers as *Maria Marten*, *Sweeney Todd* and *East Lynne*, Williams tried to draw in the public with plays which had such provocative titles as *What are Women For?*, *Married Love* and *Ruined*. (In the same bill as the last, there was a sketch called *The Young Man from Plaistow who Never Saw a Woman*.)

The greatest days of the old Stratford Theatre were, however, yet to come. Having survived aerial bombardment and other hazards of the Second World War, the 'Royal' became, in the 1950s, the headquarters of Theatre Workshop, the dedicated group of professionals who owed much of their success to the vision and competence of the brilliant Joan Littlewood. After two or three seasons in which the company built up locally a small band of devoted supporters, the reputation of the Workshop started to spread abroad. In 1954, the company was invited to take its production of *Arden of Faversham* to represent Great Britain at the Paris International Drama Festival. In 1956, they toured in Norway and Sweden. In that year, they presented Brendan Behan's first play *The Quare Fellow*. This was immediately successful and attracted full houses night after night. Several of the Workshop's subsequent productions, including Behan's second play *The Hostage*, Shelagh Delaney's *A Taste of Honey*, Frank Norman and Lionel Bart's musical *Fings ain't wot they used t'be* and Wolf Mankowicz's *Make Me an Offer* were put on afterwards in the West End, where they had long and profitable runs.

The London Borough of Barking, which lies to the east of the Borough of Newham and is, in the main, on the further side of the River Roding has reunited parts of the ancient parishes of Barking and Dagenham which were once contained in the estates of the Abbey of Barking. The south of the borough is largely industrialised—the Ford factory at Dagenham, built on some 22,000 concrete piles driven into the Thames-side marshes, is one of the largest in the country. The north of the borough contains one of London's most remarkable suburbs, the 'Becontree Housing Estate'.

This estate was brought into existence shortly after the First World War, when there was a serious shortage of housing in and near London, and when the slogan 'Homes Fit for Heroes' still had a compulsive appeal. To deal with the shortage, the members of the London County Council decided to take advantage of various Housing Acts which would allow them to provide houses for working-class people at rents that their tenants could afford to pay. They could not do this rapidly in their own area, so they decided to purchase land in the areas of other authorities. Becontree, designed, largely, by G. Topham Forrest, the L.C.C.'s own architect, is the most extensive of these 'cottage estates' and with its 26,822 homes qualifies for the title of the largest housing estate in the United Kingdom.

The rehousing of more than one hundred thousand people by one local authority in one place was a formidable operation. The land acquired consisted mainly of fields that had been used for market gardening. There were two or three rather decrepit country houses there, a few cottages, some trees, and long lines of broken-down hedgerow. The tenants put into the first houses to be built were regarded as 'pioneers'—colonists sent to an area that had no urban facilities at all. Many of them, even if they could not actually have been called 'slum dwellers' had never known what it was to have a home of their own before. Then, the construction of the estate continued rapidly, special railways being installed to carry the enormous quantities of material needed, most of which had to lie in huge dumps, on churned-up ground, round the few complete and tenanted houses. It must have been a very depressing time for the 'pioneers'.

Eventually, however, the estate was more or less finished, and very attractive it looked, with long lines of nicely proportioned houses and cottages built with mellow red bricks and with high roofs of attractive red tiles. Each dwelling had a garden suitable for the growing of roses, and there were wide roads, with broad grass verges on which decorative trees were planted. Now, in more affluent times, many of the householders at Becontree have purchased their homes from the local authority, and the attractive architectural unity of the place is being destroyed as bizarre 'modern' or 'mock Tudor' extensions are arbitrarily added, and pleasant brick surfaces are covered with uncongenial pebble dash.

CHAPTER EIGHT

Royal Greenwich, and Around

LONDON'S first local steam railway—the 'London and Greenwich'—was opened in 1836. The line had to be supported on a viaduct for very nearly the entire length of the trip from London Bridge to Greenwich Village. The viaduct had 878 arches, and was quite expensive to build. Trains had to run at frequent intervals on the line, and to be well filled with passengers, if they were to recover the outlay. The line acted, therefore, as a prototype for all the other suburban railways that were so soon to run into, and out of, the capital.

The passenger travelling by rail from London Bridge to Greenwich today will pass, before he reaches his destination, through the ancient shipbuilding town of Deptford, known in Saxon times as 'West Greenwich'. Deptford, the 'deep ford' over the Ravensbourne, which flows into the Thames just here, became internationally famous in Henry VIII's reign, when the king's naval dockyard produced such mightily powerful vessels as the famous warship the *Greyhound*'. Then, King Henry's daughter, Elizabeth I, brought further renown to the riverside settlement when she visited it to confer a knighthood on Sir Francis Drake, after that great seaman had circumnavigated the globe. (She went on board the *Golden Hind*, which was berthed between Watergate Street and the riverside end of Deptford Green.) Most of the later royal visitors to Deptford went, as a matter of course, to Sayes Court.

Sayes Court—commemorated, now, by the name of a street and by some public gardens in which there is one ancient mulberry tree—was the home, between the years 1652 and 1693, of the great diarist and horticulturist John Evelyn. 'Came His Majesty to honour my poor villa with his presence, viewing the gardens', wrote Evelyn in 1663 of the second King Charles. 'After dinner to Mr. Evelyn's,' recorded Samuel Pepys, two years later. 'He being abroad, we walked in his garden, and a lovely noble ground he hath indeed.' It was on one of his journeys 'abroad' from his home that Evelyn found a local lad named Grinling Gibbons who was doing some extraordinarily fine wood carving: 'That incomparable young man [he wrote] whom I had lately met with in an obscure place by meere accident as I was walking . . . near Sayes Court. I found him shut in; but looking in at the window I perceiv'd him carving that large cartoon or crucifix of Tintoret, a copy of which I had myself brought from Venice. I asked if I might enter; he opened the door civilly to me, and I saw him about such a work as for the curiosity of handling, drawing and studious exactness, I had never before seene in all my travells . . .'

Later, Evelyn brought the incomparable young man to the notice of King Charles II and Christopher Wren and, after that, Gibbons was given many important commissions including general responsibility for the choir stalls in the new St. Paul's.

After Evelyn left Sayes Court in 1693 and retired 'to the country', his house was let, first, to Admiral Benbow, and then to Peter the Great of Russia who had come to England at William III's invitation to learn the art of shipbuilding in the Deptford dockyards. The Russian ruler was hardly a model tenant: not only did he knock a hole through Evelyn's sturdily built garden wall so that he could reach his place of study without too long a walk, but he also managed to ruin Evelyn's famous holly hedge, which was more than a hundred yards long and five feet thick, by having his Imperial Self pushed through it, at least once every day, in a wheelbarrow. 'There is house full of people, and right nasty', wrote Evelyn's servant-on-the-spot, who did not like the Russian Royals, to the distant master. Imperial Peter left so much damage behind him when he went back to St. Petersburg that Christopher Wren had to be called in to estimate the cost of making his temporary London home sound again. The Lords of the Treasury paid out £150, then a very large sum, to reimburse the owner of the property for the Russian visitor's boorish behaviour.

There is little left in Deptford, today, to recall the days when kings and queens and visiting tsars walked across its well-kept swards. Now the ground groans beneath high blocks of council-owned flats. There are, however, two really splendid churches: St. Nicholas's, on Deptford Green, where the brilliant young dramatist Christopher Marlowe was buried after he had been stabbed in a drunken brawl in a Deptford tavern, and St. Paul's, built in 1730 by Wren's pupil Thomas Archer, which is one of the great masterpieces of English Baroque.

There are, also, two fascinating streets—Albury Street, well supplied with rather dilapidated early Georgian houses, and the High Street which, with its pubs, jellied eel caffs, bazaars and fruit stalls, cannot have been altered much since the wet Monday morning in March 1905 when an elderly couple named Farrow were found badly battered there, in a chandler's shop. The husband was dead. Mrs. Farrow died in hospital three days later. The motive had clearly been robbery but the criminals had been misled: the Farrows were only employees of the shop's proprietors, and there had not been much money on the premises.

What makes this case historically significant is the fact that the print of a right thumb was found on the tray of the cash box. This did not resemble the thumb print of either of the victims, or of a policeman who admitted that he had touched the tray. Scotland Yard was called in. Chief Inspector Fox, who took charge of the case, asked for an immediate check on all known criminals who lived in the Deptford area. Soon, suspicion fell on two young men, Albert and Alfred Stratton, who had already been to prison several times. The young men were arrested, and the thumb print on the tray was found to have eleven points of resemblance to Alfred's right thumb print. The police did not rest on this alone, but—and this established a legal precedent—the thumb print played a large part in the conviction of the brothers who were duly sentenced to death.

Downstream from Deptford, or 'West Greenwich', is Greenwich proper. From as far back as it is possible to survey, there seems to have been a human settlement of some kind in the neighbourhood of Greenwich's Church Street. It was certainly the main street of the medieval fishing village, and it still contains some interesting buildings, though none date back further than the end of the seventeenth century.

The parish church of St. Alphege, which gives Church Street its name was built by Nicholas Hawksmoor between 1711 and 1718 on the site of a very much older church that had been blown down in a storm. There has been a church on the site since the twelfth century at least. According to tradition, it was here that Alphege, Archbishop of Canterbury, was stoned to death in the year 1012. The Danes, who had sacked Canterbury and had carried off the

Archbishop, demanded a large ransom for his release. Alphege, held prisoner at Greenwich, courageously refused to allow his people to hand over any ransom at all, preferring to suffer a peculiarly horrible martyrdom. Henry VIII was certainly christened on this spot, and both Pepys and John Evelyn came frequently to services, Pepys writing characteristically in his *Diary*: 'By coach to Greenwich Church, where a good sermon, a fine church and a great company of handsome women.' James Wolfe, conqueror of Quebec, is buried in the Crypt.

A little to the east of the parish church, on the river bank, stood the house known as 'Bella Vista' that was built, around the year 1433, by Humphrey, Duke of Gloucester, who had been Protector of England during the childhood of his nephew King Henry VI. The house was taken down, or added to, later, by King Henry VII, so that the replacements became the great sprawling Palace of Placentia. Here, among other historical happenings, Henry VIII and Elizabeth I were born, Ann Boleyn was arrested after she had been seen signalling to her lover, Queen Elizabeth signed the death warrant of Mary Queen of Scots and Sir Walter Raleigh laid down his cloak. Almost every trace of the Palace of Placentia has long since been swept away. It was demolished, and pushed into the river, and there remains only a single undercroft or crypt constructed in the reign of King James I. There stands now, in place of the old royal dwelling, one of the finest sets of buildings in Europe.

Loveliest, perhaps, of all the treasures of Greenwich is the Queen's House, given by King James I to his wife Queen Anne of Denmark—it is said, by some, in order to restore their matrimonial harmony after a damaging series of rows. The house was designed 'in the Italian manner' by Inigo Jones, architect to the queen, who on his travels in Italy in 1601 and 1613 had studied carefully the revolutionary classical-style villas that had been recently built in that country by Andrea Palladio. Jones chose to set the queen's new house right on the main Deptford-to-Woolwich road and designed it so that it would consist of two rectangular blocks, one on each side of the public thoroughfare, with a cantilevered bridge over the road to connect the two halves of the royal residence.

Before her new home had risen above a single storey, however, Queen Anne died, and work on the house was stopped. Building was not resumed until 1632, when Charles I's wife Henrietta Maria took the place into her particular care. When the house was finished, three years later, it became the Queen's favourite residence. (Lime-washed, it was known as 'The White House'.) The furnishings included many almost priceless works of art.

After the Restoration, Charles II allowed the Queen Mother to resume residence in her old Greenwich home. By this time, however, Henrietta Maria felt in need of some more spacious accommodation, so Inigo Jones' pupil John Webb was asked to enlarge his master's building. He did this by adding two more over-the-road bridges on each side of the original bridge in the centre. For fifty more years, then, the public road passed through the house by means of a badly-lit tunnel. The place of the road is taken, today, by the twin colonnades that were commissioned in 1807, possibly it is believed, to commemorate Nelson's great victory at Trafalgar. The east and the west wings, linked to the Queen's House by the colonnades, accommodate, now, the majority of the exhibits in the world-famous National Maritime Museum. The buildings that lie between the National Maritime Museum and the river are known, today, as the Royal Naval College, and have been called that since 1873, when the College was moved there from Portsmouth, to be nearer to London.

After the armed conflict between King Charles I and his Parliament broke out in 1642, the riverside Palace of Placentia was sadly neglected. On his return from exile in 1660, King Charles II found that the old Tudor buildings, plentifully furnished with rotting timbers, were practically beyond repair, so he had them demolished, intending to build a new, up-to-date, and far more splendid palace on the same site.

The first architect to be called in to supervise this great project was John Webb. Webb designed a pleasant, three-sided court that could look out on the river, and one of the sides of this court (the 'King Charles Building') had actually been completed by 1669, when the available money ran out, and Charles, in consequence, lost all interest in the scheme.

For nearly twenty years, the partially built palace stood empty and forlorn. Then William and Mary were invited to reign in England. As William was asthmatic, and liked best to live at Kensington, away from the Thames-side fogs, the royal pair proposed that the disused building down at Greenwich should be added to, and used as a Naval Hospital, on much the same lines as the Royal Hospital (for army pensioners) that had been recently completed at Chelsea. The wounded and elderly seamen admitted to the hospital would get constant entertainment from the numbers of ships that were continually passing up and down the river—or so the good king and his wife optimistically thought.

Christopher Wren, called in as the royal architect, was enthusiastic. Assisted by Nicholas Hawksmoor, he drew up the plans and elevations of a monumental structure which would have, at its centre, a Great Hall and Chapel, surmounted by a magnificent dome. Unfortunately for the great architect, Queen Mary did not like his design. She was as fond as she could be of the Queen's House, and she had been brought up at a time when the demolition of the Palace of Placentia had produced, for those looking from the Queen's House's front windows, a totally unexpected and charming view of the river and of the countryside beyond. Wren's great building would block that view, she said, and she would not allow this to happen.

In consternation, Wren proposed that the whole of the hospital he had planned should be moved to one side, leaving the strip of ground between the Queen's House and the river entirely free. But, as this new scheme would involve the demolition of the existing wing that had been commissioned by her late lamented uncle, Queen Mary, who must have been an extraordinarily strong-minded woman, vetoed that too. She would not allow the King Charles Building to be touched.

So, the Naval Hospital as it was eventually completed was essentially a compromise. It was a collection of very grand buildings that were, and are, as Doctor Johnson observed, too much detached to make one great whole'. The veteran sailors who were installed in the hospital seem to have been affected to a melancholy extent by the overpowering grandeur of their surroundings—quarrels were frequent, and discontent over such matters as feeding and clothing made the community anything but a happy one. Again, Doctor Johnson had a shrewd comment to make: 'The buildings at Greenwich', he said, 'are far too magnificent for a place of charity.' By 1869, the number of pensioners had dwindled to a point where there seemed to be no need, any more, for the institution to continue. So, the buildings were vacated and, as we have seen, were taken over in four years' time by the Portsmouth college.

The old, walled main road that used to pass right through the Queen's House had a secondary purpose for it used to divide the grounds of the Palace of Placentia from the royal Greenwich Park that lay to the south. This park was first enclosed, under licence from the Crown, by Humphrey, Duke of Gloucester when he built 'Bella Vista', his riverside home.

Today, the park at Greenwich is one of the best loved of all the ten Royal Parks in the London area. However, the general layout of the park can hardly be said to be conspicuously successful. It was planned in 1662 at King Charles II's suggestion by André Le Notre, the great French expert at garden design. Instead of coming to England to inspect the ground he had been commissioned to beautify, Le Notre preferred to make his plans on paper, in his native country. Somehow, as he plotted his great formal avenues of trees, the Frenchman overlooked the fact that the land was not all on one level—the steep slope behind the Queen's House, which gives the park so much excitement and charm, might not even have existed as far as Le Notre was concerned. So, the grand central avenue of trees that Le Notre intended to lead up from the Blackheath entrance towards the Queen's House leads up, instead, to a blank expanse of sky, which today is somewhat polluted. From the edge of the high escarpment one can look down on the intended focal point, which is more than one hundred feet below.

In spite of this anomaly, the oaks, cedars, limes and contorted old Spanish chestnuts of the park—arranged, principally, in straight lines—give it an atmosphere, all too rare in England, of Gallic orderliness, and the lake, the flower gardens, and the Wilderness (which still contains some deer) contribute also to the park's attractions. But its most unusual feature, of course, is the Royal Observatory.

The observatory, from which some magnificent panoramic views of London and the industrial areas to the east of the City can be obtained, was commissioned by King Charles II in 1675. He gave the job of designing the building 'for the Observator's habitation and a little for Pompe', as the architect described it, to Christopher Wren. Royal money being at that time a little lacking, Wren decided to make use of the surviving foundations of an old tower that had been built in 1433 by Humphrey, Duke of Gloucester, when that astute politician planned to command the nearby approaches, by river and road, to the City of London. The cost of constructing the observatory—£520 and a penny—is said to have been met by the sale of old spoiled gunpowder.

The first 'Observator' or Astronomer Royal was the Reverend John Flamsteed, and the original building is, in consequence, often referred to as 'Flamsteed House'. Poor Flamsteed did not have a particularly happy time in his prominent post. His health had never been good since he had caught a cold, while bathing, at the age of twelve. This had left him with rheumatic aches and other chronic troubles and his health was not improved by the dedication he brought to his new duties. Moreover, although the Royal Warrant directed him 'forthwith to apply himself with the most exact care and diligence to the rectifying the tables of the motions of the heavens, and the places of the fixed stars, so as to find out the so much desired longitude of places for the perfecting the art of navigation', he found, when he was ready to move into the observatory, that it would contain no instruments of any kind, so that he would have to provide his own. His only official assistant was a 'surly silly labourer', and his stipend was so ridiculously insufficient that he could only meet the cost of procuring skilled aid and accurate instruments by taking in private pupils.

Worst of all were the rows in which Flamsteed became involved. In his attempts to achieve the aims defined for the observatory in the Royal Warrant, he fell foul of Sir Isaac Newton, who needed Flamsteed's accurate observations for substantiating his own revolutionary theory of gravity. The climax of this great and famous quarrel came when Newton and his friends published, without Flamsteed's authority, a version of the Astronomer Royal's classic study *Historia Celestis*. Flamsteed's discoveries were so 'mangled and garbled' in this publication, according to Flamsteed, that the author disowned his work. The death of Queen Anne in 1714, followed by that of the Earl of Halifax, who was Newton's patron, brought a turn of luck in Flamsteed's favour, for the new Lord Chamberlain asked the Lords of the Treasury to let Flamsteed have the remaining three hundred copies of the four hundred that had been printed. Flamsteed promptly consigned them to the flames as 'a sacrifice to Heavenly Truth'. His rooms, in the observatory, are open to the public each day, and have been appropriately furnished by the officials of the Victoria and Albert Museum.

The road that climbs up the hill from the ancient fishing village of Greenwich towards the high plateau of Blackheath—on the west side of the park—is one of the oldest thoroughfares in the London area. It had almost certainly been in use for several centuries by the time Duke Humphrey of Gloucester converted the nearby expanse of heath into a park, for he took the existing road, Crooms Hill, as one of the boundaries of his enclosure.

At the foot of Crooms Hill, today, stands the popular Greenwich Theatre, made from the building which, one hundred years ago, housed Crowder's Music Hall. Further up is the succession of splendid Georgian terraces and houses that make this road one of the most admired in the whole of England. Among the most notable of these houses is The Grange—called originally, it is thought, 'Paternoster Croft'—which in the year 1281 was included in the list of properties owned in Greenwich by the Abbey of Ghent. One of its subsequent owners, Sir William Hooker, Lord Mayor of London in the years of the Great Plague and the Fire, did a lot of rebuilding and had an elegant pavilion or 'gazebo' erected by the road. In spite of this he earned the contempt of Sir Samuel Pepys, whose description of Hooker, 'A plain, ordinary silly man I think he is, but rich . . .' is only surpassed by his assessment of Hooker's domestic economy: 'The poorest mean dirty table in a dirty house that ever I did see [of] any Sheriff of London . . .'

At the top of the rise, Crooms Hill runs out onto Black Heath, and there its name changes to 'General Wolfe Road', in honour of the British national hero whose father once lived just here, at Macartney House. 'The prettiest situated house in England', Wolfe called his father's home, and he stayed in it whenever he could, between campaigns. For four years, he courted a pretty girl called Elizabeth Lawson who lived in the White House, next door. Her parents disapproved, however, and this was one of the campaigns in which Wolfe had to admit defeat.

Chesterfield House, a little further on, was the home of the unctuous Lord Chesterfield who wrote so many letters to his son on the 'How-To-Make-Friends-and-Influence-People' theme. Chesterfield had become conscious, in the Paris of King Louis XIV, of his own lack of finish as a man of the world, and his life, thereafter, was to be devoted to the art of inspiring admiration. 'Without the desire of pleasing no man living can please. Let that desire be the spring of all your words and actions', he wrote in one of the famous letters. Samuel Johnson, who was not impressed, described the letters as teaching 'the morals of a whore, and the manners of a dancing master'. In spite of Johnson's scorn, Chesterfield's advice is still read and enjoyed today. In the year of Waterloo, the house became the official residence of the Ranger of Greenwich Park. It belongs, now, to the Greater London Council, and is used for chamber music concerts, art exhibitions and similar functions.

No longer standing, unfortunately, is another great mansion, Montague House, which used to be situated at the end of the long avenue of trees known as 'Chesterfield Walk'. Montague House vanished as the result of a piece of personal spite.

It was the home, for some years, of Caroline of Brunswick, wife of the eldest son of King George III. Soon after the birth of their only child, Princess Charlotte, in 1796 the unhappily matched couple separated and Caroline, given the sinecure post of Park Ranger, went to live in the house near Blackheath. The way she carried on in the district—entertaining dashing gentlemen from London, and that—caused great scandal and at last, in December 1805, she was accused of having given birth to a child, a boy named 'William Austin'. A committee of the Privy Council which investigated the matter acquitted her of this serious charge, though the members of the committee decided to censure her for 'levity of manners'. Excluded from the court after her husband became Prince Regent in 1811, she decided to live abroad, and was presently accused of having had 'adulterous intercourse' with her Italian courier Bartolomeo Pergami, with whom she had plainly become infatuated. She returned to England in 1820 in a vain attempt to claim her rights as the Queen, but the house in which she had lived when she was Greenwich's Park Ranger was no longer there. Her unforgiving husband, loathing everything that could possibly be associated with her, had had it razed to the ground. A stone bath that she had had built, in one of her gardens is the only tangible reminder of Caroline's residence which remains on the site. It can be seen, now, in a corner of the park.

The land immediately to the east of Greenwich Park has not as many fine mansions to show as that to the west, but there are at least two very unusual buildings that are worth more than a cursory glance. Vanbrugh Castle (sometimes called 'The Bastille'), is a pseudo-medieval fortress designed for his own use by Sir

John Vanbrugh, who worked as Surveyor to the Royal Naval Hospital between 1717 and 1726, and 'Woodlands', in Mycenae Road, was built in 1774 as a country villa for John Julius Angerstein, the wealthy financier whose pictures formed, after his death, the nucleus of the National Gallery collection. 'Woodlands' contained the first central heating system to be installed in this country since the days of the Romans for there was a 'hot room', heated by a furnace in the cellar, that was designed to extend Mr. Angerstein's life. King George III, who went to dine at Woodlands with Mr. Angerstein, said that he did not think much of this installation. He preferred 'a good coal fire'. In spite of this lack of royal enthusiasm, Mr. Angerstein lived to be ninety-seven.

A little to the east of the Royal Naval College, at the end of the Embankment Walk, stands the last of the famous Greenwich riverside taverns, the 'Trafalgar'. This tavern was designed by Joseph Kay who was Surveyor to the Royal College, and was built in 1837. The 'Trafalgar' was celebrated throughout Queen Victoria's reign for the excellent whitebait dinners that were served there, the fish usually being washed down with iced punch or champagne. (In his *Dictionary of the Thames*, published in 1888, Charles Dickens' son said, 'There is no next morning headache like that which follows a Greenwich dinner'.) At the end of each parliamentary session until 1883 it was customary for the whole Cabinet to journey to Greenwich to partake of one of those dinners. The Liberals favoured the 'Trafalgar'. The Tories preferred the 'Ship', which stood near the western end of the Embankment Walk, and which was destroyed during the Second World War. Charles Dickens the Elder who, with his literary and other friends, used to patronise the 'Trafalgar' frequently, tried to immortalise the tavern in the pages of *Our Mutual Friend*. He chose it, as the setting for Bella Wilfer's wedding feast.

The 'Trafalgar' was closed in 1915 when, with the decline of trade, Greenwich had become a temporarily depressed area. There were plans that the old place should be demolished, so that flats could be built on the spot, but these were frustrated by the outbreak of the Second World War. The tavern was re-opened in 1965 and now serves excellent meals again.

Since the Second World War, two historic vessels have been given, on the riverside ground at Greenwich, permanent places of retirement. The *Cutty Sark* has been at Greenwich since 1954.

Built in 1869 at Dumbarton on the Clyde, this great clipper was one of a breed of sailing ships whose speed and reliability became proverbial. There was an enormous amount of rivalry between the owners of these ships and the journey back to England from China with the first freights of the new season's tea became an annual race causing a great deal of excitement and attracting some very profitable publicity. Fully rigged, the *Cutty Sark* spread over 30,000 square feet of sail. As John Masefield, the Poet Laureate, commented in an explanatory tablet:

> They mark our passage as a race of men
> Earth will not see such ships as these again

Early in 1968, it was decided that Sir Francis Chichester's *Gipsy Moth IV* should be preserved in Greenwich, near the last of the great trading clippers. The story of Francis Chichester's single-handed journey round the world, with its hazards and disasters, all successfully overcome by a mixture of skill and incredible tenacity, is too well-known to bear prolonged repetition. The trip, which started and finished at Plymouth, took him just nine months and one day. After a short rest, Chichester brought the *Gipsy Moth* back to Greenwich, and there, on 7 July, 1967 Queen Elizabeth II knighted the brave sailor by the water gate of the Royal Naval College, using the very sword with which her ancestor Elizabeth I had knighted Francis Drake just a little way upstream at Deptford.

Woolwich, which lies on the south bank of the Thames downstream from Greenwich, is usually regarded as a poor relation of its royal neighbour. The town had, once, a famous naval dockyard —King Henry VIII's *Great Harry* was built there, and King Charles I's *Sovereign of the Seas*—but this was closed before the end of the nineteenth century, and, since the Second World War the Woolwich Military Arsenal has also been largely run down. The Royal Military Academy, in Academy Road, was established in 1741 'for instructing the gentlemen belonging to the train of artillery', but the Academy was closed down in 1945 and amalgamated with the Royal Military College at Sandhurst. The buildings, designed by James Wyatt, now accommodate the Royal Artillery Museum.

On the other side of Woolwich Common, near the Royal Artillery Barracks, is another museum housed in a curious Rotunda. This building was originally a vast tent that was put up by the Prince Regent in 1814 in the gardens of Carlton House to celebrate the victory of the Allies over Napoleon Buonaparte. (The Prince had invited all the allied sovereigns to come to London to attend a lavish triumphal reception and to confer about the consequences of their success, and he wanted a rather large and unusual pavilion in which they could meet.) Unfortunately for the Prince Regent, his joy—and theirs—was premature. Napoleon, as we all know, escaped from captivity and the war had to continue for another year. In 1819, the Prince gave orders that the tent should be taken to Woolwich to house 'the military curiosities usually preserved in the Repository of the Royal Artillery'. In 1822, John Nash, who had designed the tent originally, was given the job of making the structure permanent. He did this most successfully by adding a central support and by building an outer shell, in which a polygonal yellow brick wall supports a steep concave copper roof.

The old royal palace of Eltham still stands on the high ground to the south of Woolwich, where London's suburbs start to take on a countrified air. Edward IV's Great Hall, which has not been changed in any major respect during the five centuries that have elapsed since it was built, has the third largest hammerbeam roof in the whole of the country. (It is beaten only by those at Westminster and at Christchurch, Oxford.) King Henry VIII was the last English monarch to live at Eltham, and though he deserted it and went to live at Greenwich the fabric of the palace was kept up until the reign of King Charles I. Then, during the Civil War, the place was pillaged and left in a derelict state. For more than two hundred years, the remnants of the palace were used as farm buildings, the Great Hall being turned into a hay barn. Since 1859, when its worth was once again recognised, the palace has been sympathetically restored.

CHAPTER NINE

Blackheath, Lewisham, and Parts of the London Borough of Bromley

PART of the great expanse of open ground known now as 'Blackheath' lies in the London Borough of Greenwich. Part lies in the London Borough of Lewisham. The division is an arbitrary one, created by twentieth-century bureaucrats. If Blackheath can be said to be convincingly divided at all, it would be by the great Roman road, Watling Street, that runs across it, taking travellers from Dover to London, and *vice versa.* In the past few centuries this important thoroughfare has been known, in the vicinity of Blackheath, as 'Shooter's Hill Road'. Charles Dickens chose Shooter's Hill as the proper setting for the start of the adventures in his sensational novel *A Tale of Two Cities*:

> It was the Dover road that lay, on a Friday night late in November, before the first of the persons with whom this history has business. The Dover road lay, as to him, beyond the Dover mail, as it lumbered up Shooter's Hill. He walked uphill in the mire by the side of the mail as the rest of the passengers did; not because they had the least relish for walking exercise under the circumstances, but because the hill, and the harness, and the mud, and the mail, were all so heavy, that the horses had three times already come to a stop, besides once drawing the coach across the road, with the mutinous intent of taking it back to Blackheath. Reins and whip and coachman and guard, however, in combination, had read that article of war which forbad a purpose otherwise strongly in favour of the argument, that some brute animals are endued with Reason; and the team had capitulated and returned to their duty . . .

Throughout the ages, until quite recently, the 'Black' or 'Bleak' Heath was a wild and overgrown waste, covered with dense furze and bracken, that no sane person would venture to cross alone without a sense of misgiving, and weapons. As late as 1816, the relatives of a Doctor Bramley, who were on their way to Paris, drove across the heath with a pistol pointed at their driver because they suspected that he might wish to land them in the clutches of his confederates who, they thought, were lurking in the gorse.

The heath originally extended from Blackheath Hill to Shooter's Hill and from Kidbrooke to Greenwich. This wide expanse of unpopulated ground was an ideal spot for the assembly of riotous throngs and for the disposition of the armies that were required to deal with them.

On Black Heath in 1381, for instance, Wat Tyler collected his hundred thousand supporters who were marching on London from their native county of Kent to protest about the iniquitous taxes that were being levied at the time. Having failed to obtain an audience with King Richard II who was in his barge off Greenwich, Tyler led his men into Southwark and from there across London Bridge into the City. The king met the Kentish men at Smithfield on Saturday, 15 June. During an argument with one of the king's attendants, Tyler was attacked and badly wounded by the Mayor of London, which brought the Great Rebellion to a speedy and ignominious end.

On Black Heath, too, in 1415 King Henry V, returning victorious from the Battle of Agincourt, was welcomed back to London by the City's Lord Mayor. Jack Cade, alias 'John Mortimer, Captain of Kent', led his protesting rebels from Ashford to Black Heath thirty-five years after that, and camped on the heath, retreating a week later when the king (Henry VI) advanced on them with his troops. Overtaken at Sevenoaks, Cade's men managed to defeat part of the king's army. They then made their way back to London, where they put the Lord Treasurer to death, as well as his hated son-in-law William Crowmer, who was Sheriff of Kent. The people of London quickly tired of Cade's lawlessness, and his supporters had to withdraw.

Of all the historical figures who are said to have played a part in the story of the Black Heath, none has been more grievously misrepresented, surely, than poor Anne of Cleves (1515–57). On the first day of January 1540, King Henry VIII went towards Rochester to meet her for the first time, it having been arranged that she was to come to England from the Low Countries to become his fourth wife. The story that they met on the Black Heath, and that Henry found her immediately displeasing and 'no better than a Flanders mare', though plausible, is supported only by the flimsiest of evidence—it rests, principally, on reports made by Thomas Cromwell, in the Tower of London, six months later, when he was desperately trying to earn himself a royal pardon. It is more likely that since the marriage had become a political embarrassment, its validity had to be questioned in parliament, so that it could be annulled. Anne, it is known, agreed to this arrangement, and was rewarded with lands worth £4000 a year which she was to keep on condition she stayed in England. She settled down quite happily and was soon trying on, with delight, a new dress every day.

Less than a century after Anne of Cleves crossed the Black Heath on her way to London, the game of golf was played on the heath, it is believed, for the first time in England. (It had been played, earlier, in Scotland, and it was brought from there by the courtiers of King James I.) Certainly, the Royal Blackheath Golf Club, founded in 1608, is the oldest in the country. It would be interesting to see the club's early records, but unfortunately these do not exist any longer, having been destroyed, it is said, by a fire at the end of the eighteenth century. A 'bet book' commencing July 1791 has been preserved, however, and it shows that some of the wagers made on the games at that time were quite substantial: 'Saturday, 9th July, 1791. Mr. Pitcaithly bets Capt. Faithfull one gallon of claret that he drives the Short Hole in Three strokes, six times in ten—to be played for the first time he comes to Blackheath—after the Annual Day. Lost and paid by Mr. Pitcaithly the 10th September.'

Until the year 1844, the course extended over five holes only, and was situated near the south-west corner of Greenwich Park. Parts of the heath were then being extensively quarried for gravel, and the golfers had to avoid some extraordinary hazards. There are, today, twenty-eight football pitches and thirteen cricket pitches on the heath, all of which are fully used.

The present shape of Blackheath is due to various enclosures, authorised and otherwise, which over the centuries have reduced its size. Humphrey, Duke of Gloucester's enclosure, made under licence from the king, has already been referred to. Then, as the palace at Greenwich became increasingly popular with the Royal

Family, other noblemen started to build their handsome private residences round the heath which, in consequence, gradually started to lose its desolate and seemingly endless appearance.

A big step forward in this direction was taken around the year 1674 when the three great mansions at the top of Crooms Hill—known, later, as Macartney House, Chesterfield House and Montague House—were constructed on ground taken quietly and illegally from the Crown by Andrew Snape, who was King Charles II's Serjeant Farrier. In the previous year, Admiral George Legge (later, 'Baron Dartmouth') who was to become one of James II's principal advisers, had purchased the 'Manor with the rectory, church parsonage and advowson of the Vicarage of Lewisham'. The manor included the greater part of the Black Heath, and Legge managed to obtain a royal charter which would allow him to hold a fair on the heath every May and October. John Evelyn went to one, from Sayes Court: 'May 1, 1683, I went to Blackheath to see the new faire, being the first procured by Lord Dartmouth. This was the first day, pretended for the sale of cattle, but I think, in truth, to enrich the new tavern at the bowling green, erected by Snape, His Majesty's farrier, a man full of projects. There appeared nothing but an innumerable assembly of drinking people from London, pedlars etc., and I suppose it is too near London to be of any greate use to the country . . .'

Evelyn's suppositions were to be proved wrong. The fair on Blackheath was to flourish for another two centuries, finally ceasing in 1872.

By 1695, Baron Dartmouth, copying the enterprising Snape, had put up eleven new houses at the west end of the heath, in and near what is now 'Dartmouth Row'. Some of these beautifully proportioned buildings still exist, among them, Spencer House and Perceval House, which were built as one dwelling at that time. They were still one single residence in 1812, when the Prime Minister of England, Spencer Perceval, who spent much of his time there, was shot, as he was leaving the House of Commons, by the distraught John Bellingham. Bellingham, who was forty-one years old, had lost nearly all his money when his business in Russia had failed. For some time, he had been petitioning the government to take up his case and to obtain some proper compensation for him, but the evasiveness of the various officials with whom he had had to deal, and their procrastinations, had at last, it is thought, unhinged poor Bellingham's mind. After Perceval died the unhappy wretch was tried and sentenced to death.

The beautiful village of Blackheath, which is all ups and downs, with quaint little alleys and passageways, was virtually non-existent in the year 1745. The place started to grow towards the end of the eighteenth century, building beginning, principally, in the part now known as 'Collins Square'. (Then, it was known as 'Dowagers Bottom'.) At the Bottom, several small cross routes joined. One ran along the south side of the heath. Another led up from Lee Green, which then consisted of only a few cottages, an inn, and a windmill. The third followed the course of the River Ravensbourne and was called 'Lewisham Lane'. On the north side of the great Wricklemarsh Estate, in a dell, there were a few isolated buildings of which some survivors can be seen today in Tranquil Vale.

Blackheath Village, then, continued to grow steadily as the nineteenth century wore on. By 1820, Tranquil Vale and Montpelier Road were in existence, though many of the buildings in them were afterwards altered or replaced. The opening of the North Kent Railway stations at Blackheath and Lewisham in 1849 led to a rapid increase in housing, but still the special quality of the district was not spoiled, and the architectural character of the village, with its large houses built in the Georgian, Regency and Victorian periods, interspersed with groups of smaller dwellings, some old, some new, is now widely regarded as unique.

Among the most notorious of all the worthy people who felt the urge to live in 'polite' Blackheath during the nineteenth century were Mr. and Mrs. Samuel Smiles.

Samuel Smiles was born and brought up in Haddington, East Lothian, and trained as a surgeon in Edinburgh. In May 1838, when he was twenty-five, the young man became dissatisfied with the meagre living he was earning by treating the poor folk of Haddington, and he went to Leyden, thinking that a foreign degree might help him a bit in his professional life. After touring Western Europe, he returned to England, and went to London. Soon, he was offered the Editorship of the *Leeds Times*. After that, he gave up doctoring altogether, and, in 1845, he became assistant to the Secretary of the new Leeds and Thirsk Railway. When he was later appointed Secretary of the South Eastern Railway Company, he settled with his wife in Blackheath, first at 8 Glenmohr Terrace,

Greenwich Way and later in Granville Park. They lived at Blackheath, all told, for twenty years.

World-wide fame came to Samuel Smiles in 1858 when he decided to publish, at his own expense and risk, a series of talks that he had prepared for young men who needed encouragement. 'Heaven helps those who help themselves', was Smiles' theme. The book, which he called *Self-Help*, was a fantastic success, being translated into French, Russian, German, Italian, Swedish, Dutch, Spanish, Czech, Croatian, Turkish, Egyptian, Tamil, Murati, Gujerati, Hindustani, Canares, Magyar, Siamese, Armenian, Pali and other languages too numerous to mention. With the huge profits that rolled in from the sales of *Self-Help*, Smiles had a comfortable mansion built, which from its rear windows commanded magnificent views of the still-countrified Lewisham Valley.

In their new home, his wife and children were able to give some notable parties, tempered, under Samuel's influence, by a proper regard for economy. Champagne would not normally be served in the Smiles home, as it was in so many other grand houses at Blackheath. Instead, Mrs. Smiles offered coffee, music and conversation. ('Thus we do it cheap and genteel', reported her husband.) As Samuel went to great pains to provide unusual scientific entertainments, in addition to the music, the parties seem to have been enjoyed in spite of the austerity of the fare provided. As the great man put it, in one of his letters: 'Miss Browne was there and she, though very young, is an exquisite pianiste and astonished everyone with her pianoforte performance. Charlie Davis presided at two microscopes, and you have no idea how sweetly he brought the girls' eyes up to the binocular, focusing them on the ear of a mouse or the toe of a whelk . . .'

The Smiles moved from Blackheath in 1874, when all their children had left them—in one of Samuel Smiles' grand-daughter's words, 'through death, or marriage, or discontent'. They went to the more fashionable village of Kensington, because it was a little more convenient for London. They could afford to live there in true Victorian luxury because *Self-Help* was selling even better, sixteen years after publication, than it had done when it first came out.

Until the middle of the nineteenth century, Lewisham, two miles or so to the south-west of Blackheath Village, consisted merely of the few shops and cottages that made up the single street, interspersed with a few larger houses standing in their own grounds. The single street, now the High Street, was unpaved, and a stream with elm trees on its banks running down its western side gave it a rural appearance 'not without points of beauty' (to quote the words of a Victorian guide). There were small hamlets at Perry Hill, Sydenham and South End. Lee was a parish of parks and farms, the houses being mostly grouped in the Old Road and at Lee Green.

Towards the end of a July day, in 1837, some labourers saw and picked up an extraordinary contraption in one of the fields at Lee. While they were wondering what it was, a gentleman on horseback rode up and told them that they had found the shattered remains of a remarkable new invention called a 'parachute' and that the body of a man must be somewhere in the neighbourhood. The labourers did not believe that this could be true. To convince them, the gentleman explained what a parachute was and offered five guineas to whoever should find the body. All, then, started to search diligently.

After crossing four fields, they heard groans from one at Burnt Ash, and going in that direction they found an unfortunate Mr. Cocking literally dashed to pieces. As they loosened his cravat, he breathed his last in their arms. They took him quickly, then, to the 'Tiger's Head' Inn at Lee, where four medical men attended. The doctors' services were given in vain.

Mr. Cocking was an artist by profession, but as a hobby he had maintained a keen interest in scientific matters. Ballooning had particularly interested him—as it had interested many adventurous people for some years before this—and he had studied the various parachute descents that had been made, usually with disastrous results.

Cocking made his own ascent at Vauxhall Gardens, the ingenious umbrella-like 'descending machine' he had invented being attached to the great Nassau Balloon flown by the famous balloonists Messrs. Green and Spencer so that he was carried below them. (There was a contrivance which ensured that he could be taken up into their basket in case of an emergency. There was a tube, too, which would convey ballast discarded from the balloon without letting it come into contact with the parachute below, and a 'communication tube' through which the balloonists and the parachutist could talk with one another once they were up in the air.) A large and excited crowd watched the ascent.

Mr. Cocking had a theory. He believed that the greater the distance he had to fall, the greater would be the atmospheric pressure under his parachute and the easier, therefore, would be his descent. To achieve his object, Messrs. Green and Spencer had to get rid of 400 lbs. more ballast than they would normally have done, and even then they only managed to reach a height of 5,000 feet—they were still three thousand feet lower than the elevation Mr. Cocking required. Eventually, however, Messrs. Green and Spencer told Mr. Cocking through their speaking tube that it would not be possible for them to get him up as high as he desired in sufficient time for him to make his descent by the light of day. On hearing that, Mr. Cocking said: 'Then I shall very soon leave you; but tell me whereabouts I am.' Mr. Spencer, who had a few minutes before he caught a glimpse of the earth, answered: 'We appear to be on a level with Greenwich.' Mr. Cocking then declined an offer to haul himself up into the car of the balloon, and after assuring Messrs. Green and Spencer that he had never felt more comfortable or more happy in his life, freed his parachute and himself from the Great Nassau. Relieved of their weight, the balloon shot upwards with the velocity of a sky rocket. 'For a few moments the parachute descended so beautifully and preserved its position so steadily, notwithstanding its fearful motion', said an observer on the ground, 'I thought it might reach the ground in safety, and felt relieved.' The gentleman on horseback was a Mr. Underwood of Regent Street, who had followed the course of the balloon all the way from London.

At the Inquest held at the 'Tiger's Head' tavern, it was denied that the proprietor of the inn had 'exhibited the corpse of the lamented individual', but in reply to a question from the Coroner the publican admitted that he had received £10 in sixpences from persons who wished to see the mangled body.

The south-west corner of the London Borough of Lewisham and the land near it in the adjoining Borough of Bromley was virtually unknown to Londoners until the old South Eastern Railway Company started to operate in 1839. The company's line ran from London Bridge through Forest Hill—then, as its name implies, delightfully wooded—to Croydon and beyond. When stations were made on the line at Penge and Anerley, small select suburban communities soon started to appear around them. Fine, solid villas were built, standing in respectably large gardens, and these districts became fashionable and highly desirable places in which the comfortably-off could live. (When the first house was built at Anerley, in the early 1800s, the owner, a Scotsman, gave it the name of 'Ainley' meaning 'solitary' or 'alone', and it was from this that the district took its name.)

Then, when Prince Albert's Great Exhibition of the Arts and Sciences closed in 1852, and the huge iron and glass pavilion that had been specially built to house it in Hyde Park was dismantled, it was decided that the whole structure should be re-erected on an elevated two hundred acre site in the north-west corner of Penge. The big house named Penge Place was pulled down to make room for the vast structure, and 6,400 workmen were employed for two years in making the move. In 1854, its first year on its new site, the 'Crystal Palace'—as it came to be affectionately called—attracted 1,250,000 visitors and the wide park that surrounded it, with its world-famous collection of life-size models of prehistoric beasts, soon became one of the most popular places to visit in the whole of South London. Suburbs started to sprout rapidly round Penge, after that.

But the Crystal Palace was not to stay unharmed for ever in its new setting. The Tropical Courts were destroyed by fire in 1866. Then, on 1 December, 1936, most of the rest of the Palace went up in a spectacular conflagration that attracted, in vain, ninety fire engines and more than five hundred firemen. Only the tall end towers were left and these, in their turn, had to be demolished in 1941 because they were acting as landmarks for enemy aircraft.

For more than ten years after that, the grounds of the Palace remained in a forlorn and neglected state, but they started a new lease of life in 1952 when they were taken over by the London County Council. Plans were made, as quickly as possible, for turning the land into a National Recreation Centre. Among other amenities, the Centre today offers a main sports hall with a covered running track, gymnasia, tennis courts, swimming pools, an open air arena, a ski-slope, and a hostel for visiting athletes. A children's zoo has been opened in the grounds, and the 'prehistoric animals' have been given a face-lift.

Beckenham and Bromley, to the east of Penge, are both old settlements—Bromley was once a small market town—that have rather lost any special appeal they may have had since they have been turned into what the guide books describe as 'favoured residential areas'. A little to the east and a little to the south of Bromley lies Petts Wood, a comparatively new suburb so-called because of the wood that lies on its northern boundary, and which is believed to have been planted by members of the Pett family who were England's greatest shipbuilders during the reigns of the Tudor and Stuart sovereigns. After the fall of France in 1940, two very distinguished visitors, General and Madame de Gaulle, spent the first months of their enforced exile from their native country in a house in Birchwood Road.

CHAPTER TEN

Battersea, Clapham and Balham

IF the suburbs immediately to the south-east of the City of London have been given a special air of importance for several centuries by the royal figures who have lived in them, the suburbs immediately to the south-west of the City of Westminster have been dominated during the same period of time by people with money and powerful personalities who have not actually been crowned.

Battersea lies just over the Thames from Chelsea, and throughout the Middle Ages was an up-river retreat for the really grand, who found the quietness of this stretch of rural riverside refreshing after the noise and turmoil of the capital. The Archbishops of York had a house here from about 1480 onwards, which they used whenever they needed to be near the Court. When one of them, Archbishop Holgate, was committed to the Tower by Queen Mary in 1513, the officers who arrested him raided the Battersea house and took away £300 in gold coin, 1,600 pieces of plate, a mitre of fine gold set with diamonds and sapphires, some 'very valuable rings', and many other treasures. The site of York House is covered, now, by Messrs. Prices' extensive candle factory, but its memory is perpetuated by York Road, which leads down to the river.

During the greater part of the seventeenth and eighteenth centuries, Battersea was ruled very effectively by members of the St. John family, whose seat stood on the banks of the Thames adjoining the churchyard. The most noted of all the Battersea St. Johns was Henry, Viscount Bolingbroke, who was baptised in Battersea Church in 1678 and who led the Tories, in the days of Queen Anne, as Secretary of State and Secretary of War. 'His attachment to Queen Anne exposed him to a long and severe persecution; he bore it with firmness of mind,' records his epitaph, in the church. (It was written by Bolingbroke himself.)

Bolingbroke returned in 1743 from voluntary exile and took possession of the family riverside estates. He spent his time at Battersea in polite retirement, entertaining his friends and acquaintances, and composing elegant pamphlets. When he found out that Alexander Pope had secretly printed 1,500 copies of his *Essay on a Patriot King*, Bolingbroke is said to have seized the lot and to have burned them, in a glorious bonfire, outside the windows of his Battersea home. In 1751, Bolingbroke died of a malignant growth on his face. Even as late as 1816, an elderly resident of Battersea declared that she remembered Lord Bolingbroke well: 'He used to ride out every day in his chariot, and had a black patch on his cheek, with a large wart over one of his eyebrows.' The greater part of the Battersea manor house was demolished in 1778, but a small remnant was left standing, and this, which included the famous 'Cedar Room', was incorporated eventually in Messrs. Mayhews' mills, which were built round it, the walls and floors remaining as part of the fabric of the mills until 1926 when, being judged to be unsafe, they were demolished. Falcon Road, which connects St. John's Hill and Lavender Hill with Battersea Park Road and the riverside, gets its name from the bird of prey used as a heraldic crest by the St. John family. The district still has a busy inn called 'The Falcon'.

Between the years 1750 and 1756, a new industry was developed at Battersea. The instigator, Alderman Stephen-Theodore Janssen, produced at his manufactory that stood between York Road and the river, a variety of small goods made from copper, on which an opaque ground, usually white, was laid. The painted decoration applied to this ground in enamelled colours gave Janssen's goods the name by which they were usually known—'Battersea enamels'. They looked as if they were made of the finest porcelain, but felt quite different to the touch.

For some time past, artists and craftsmen had been wondering whether it would not be possible to transfer a design from an engraved plate on to paper, and from there to a properly prepared surface on which it could be fixed or 'fired'. Several innovators claimed that they were the first to try this method, but it is now generally agreed that Simon Ravenet (1706–74), the accomplished engraver who worked with William Hogarth, was, in fact, the real inventor. He introduced the technique, which was to be of enormous importance in the ceramic industry, in Janssen's factory at Battersea, or so it is believed.

In spite of the exquisite quality of the work produced for sale by Janssen, the Alderman, like so many other punctilious tradesmen

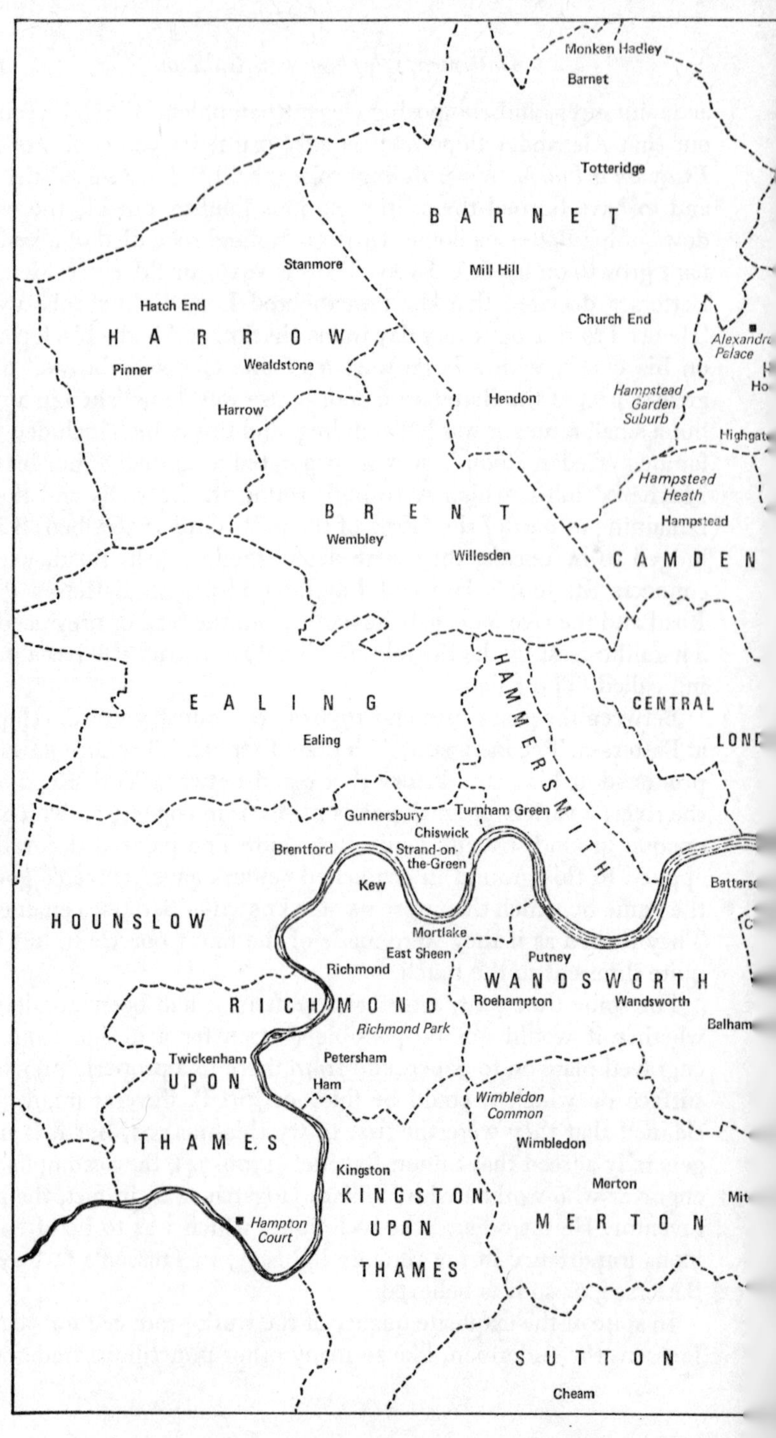

Monken Hadley
Barnet
Totteridge
BARNET
Stanmore
Mill Hill
Hatch End
Church End
HARROW
Alexandra
Palace
Pinner
Wealdstone
Hampstead
Garden
Suburb
Hendon
Harrow
Highgate
Hampstead
Heath
BRENT
Hampstead
Wembley
Willesden
CAMDEN
HAMMERSMITH
EALING
CENTRAL
Ealing
Gunnersbury
Turnham Green
Chiswick
Brentford
Strand-on-
the-Green
Kew
HOUNSLOW
Mortlake
East Sheen
Putney
Richmond
WANDSWORTH
Roehampton
Wandsworth
RICHMOND
Richmond Park
Balham
Twickenham
Petersham
UPON
Ham
Wimbledon
Common
THAMES
Wimbledon
Kingston
Merton
KINGSTON
Hampton
Court
UPON
MERTON
THAMES
SUTTON
Cheam

nfield
FIELD
Epping Forest
Chingford
Edmonton
WALTHAM
FOREST
Woodford
REDBRIDGE
Green
Tottenham
GEY
Walthamstow
Wanstead
Ilford
HACKNEY
Barking
BARKING
Stratford
East Ham
TOWER
HAMLETS
West Ham
NEWHAM
ver Thames
SOUTHWARK
Woolwich
GREENWICH
Greenwich
Deptford
Blackheath
Lewisham
Eltham
LEWISHAM
Crystal
Palace
Bromley
BROMLEY
1 ½ 0 1 2
miles

before and after him, went bankrupt. The advertisement of the sale of his goods on this unhappy occasion mentions: 'Beautiful enamels, coloured and uncoloured, of the new manufactory carried on at York House, Battersea, and never yet exhibited to public view, consisting of snuff-boxes of all sizes, of a great variety of patterns; of square and oval pictures of the Royal Family, history, and other pleasing subjects, very proper subjects for the cabinets of the curious; bottle tickets, with chains, for all sorts of liquors, and of different subjects; watch cases, tooth-picks cases, coat and sleeve buttons, crosses, and other curiosities, mostly mounted in metal, double gilt . . .' Janssen's 'curiosities', today, fetch astronomic prices on the rare occasions on which they appear in the sale rooms.

By the beginning of the nineteenth century, Battersea had definitely lost 'tone'. The wealthy and cultured families who had been living there had left, and the riverside fields once owned by the St. Johns had become a dreary waste, frequented principally by gypsies, roughs and bad characters and used—since they were remote, and lonely—for prize fighting, organised dog fights, and other disorderly pastimes. In March 1829 a memorable duel took place on the fields between the great Duke of Wellington and the Earl of Winchelsea. The Duke fired first, and missed his target. Winchelsea then fired into the air and immediately afterwards tendered an apology to the Duke. (It was Winchelsea's refusal to do so, previously, that had led to the quarrel in the first place.) So, both parties went away unscathed, and with their honours more or less satisfied.

By 1852, the scenes that were taking place on the riverside ground had become so shocking that The Law had to step in. The fairs that had been held by the river were suppressed, and the fields were effectively policed. Six years later, the place, cleaned up and properly organised, was opened freely to the public again as 'Battersea Park'. Today, it is one of London's most popular places of outdoor entertainment. It has Big Dippers, All The Fun of The Fair and an annual Easter Parade. The St. Johns would hardly have been able to imagine that such common frivolities could ever take place on their ground.

By one of the strange ironies that crop up every now and then to redress a social imbalance, Battersea, which was for so long a strictly aristocratic preserve, became, once the aristocrats moved out, a place in which the Left Wing took root, and flourished exceedingly. One of the first local men to raise some serious questions about the way the world happened to be organised at that time, from an economic point of view, was a Mr. Thomas Atkinson.

Thomas Atkinson served his apprenticeship with George Stephenson, who was the Great Founding Father of all the railways. (Young Thomas actually helped the great George and his son Robert to build their historic award-winning steam locomotive *The Rocket*. At the time Thomas' indentures of apprenticeship were signed in 1825 there was not one single mile of railway on earth on which any such mechanically propelled vehicle had ever travelled, to provide a regular public service.)

Unfortunately or fortunately, according to one's point of view, the Stephensons' handy lad came to hear about the new associations known as 'Trades Unions', and he heartily approved of them. As he grew to manhood, Thomas Atkinson became involved in many fierce struggles on behalf of his fellow workers. On one of these occasions, in 1836, a warrant was actually issued for his arrest. To escape from the hefty Peelers who were looking for him, Atkinson rowed himself down the Thames on a tempestuous night and got himself picked up, somewhere down-river, by a vessel bound for Hull, and safety.

In 1874, Atkinson helped to organise a 'strike', then a comparatively new exercise in social relations, at the Battersea Engineering Works of the London, Chatham and Dover Railway Company. From that moment on, he was a marked man, loathed by all capitalists, and virtually unable to obtain any rewardable employment. Being, happily, by that time sixty-three years old, the ageing socialist agreed to retire from business and to draw, from then on, his lawful superannuation allowance from the Engineers' Association. On this small pension he managed somehow to live until 1907. Then, when he had reached the ripe old age of ninety-six, steps were taken to raise a fund for his benefit. These steps included the holding of a Grand Concert at the Battersea Town Hall. Among the Members of Parliament present in the crowded audience on that jolly occasion was another eminent Battersea agitator, Mr. John Burns, the President of the Local Government Board.

John Burns was born in 1858 in a dreary little house in Simpson Street, in South Lambeth. He was the sixteenth child of a man with a very small wage. While he was still a boy, the family moved to Lavender Hill. By 1885, Burns was campaigning busily for social reform. As a result of a great meeting held in Trafalgar Square in April of that year on behalf of the starving unemployed of London, he was tried at the Old Bailey on an indictment that charged him with seditious conspiracy. The jury, having heard the evidence, decided that though the language used by Messrs. Burns and Champion (another defendant) was highly inflammatory and greatly to be condemned, the defendants, on the whole of the facts laid before the court, should be acquitted of seditious intent. Burns, after that, was the socialists' hero.

The severe crisis dragged on through 1885 and 1886, with Burns busily agitating on behalf of the poor and oppressed. On one famous occasion, the man from Battersea led an excited crowd through the West End, carrying a red flag and waving it wildly. At the windows of the Carlton, the Thatched House, and other gentlemen's clubs, on that stimulating day, volleys of stones were thrown.

The climax to Burns' efforts came on 13 November, 1887—a day known thereafter by all London Radicals as 'Bloody Sunday'—when immense crowds attempted to enter Trafalgar Square, which had been sealed off by the police. Burns was arrested and, at a subsequent trial at the Old Bailey, was found guilty of unlawful assault and sentenced to six weeks' imprisonment.

Burns may have been a great fighter against social injustice, but he was also undoubtedly an impatient and jealous man who was not happy unless he, himself, was the centre of attention. Beatrice Webb, who was an astute judge of character, wrote in 1893 of Burns: 'So long as he does not fear any diminution of his personal prestige, his judgment is very fine.' Later, she referred to his 'immense self-conceit and assurance'. By 1907, she was writing of him, 'John Burns has become a monstrosity'. Joseph Burgess, author of *Reminiscences of a Socialist Agitator*, recalled in 1911:

> I remember seeing, from my seat at the press table at the Cardiff Trades Congress, Burns pulling the coat-tails of an American fraternal delegate. This was the first time fraternal delegates from America had attended the British Trades Union Congress. They had travelled more than three thousand miles to deliver their message. But Burns could not abide to hear it out. The

first delegate was not on his feet more than ten minutes before Burns tugged at him to sit down. I once discussed this habit of Burns with Will Crooks, when he told me he never by any chance sat next to Burns on a platform. 'I always', Crooks said, 'note where Burns is sitting, and then get as far away from him as possible' . . .

In 1914, John Burns moved from working-class Battersea to a comfortably large house, called 'Alverstoke', on the north side of Clapham Common. He had become by that time almost respectable.

Clapham, from which some magnificent views could be obtained before the district became so heavily built up, remained for rather longer than Battersea a socially desirable place in which to live. In the seventeenth century, Sir Dennis Gauden, Victualler to the Navy and Sheriff of London, had a palatial house here, with an estate of over four hundred acres. On 25 July, 1663, Samuel Pepys went to see him: 'I resolved to go to Clapham . . . When I came there the first thing was [for Sir Dennis] to show me his house which is almost built. I find it very regular and finely contrived and the gardens and offices about it as convenient and full of variety as ever I saw in my life. It is true he hath been censured for laying out so much money, but he tells me he built it for his brother who is since dead . . .'

Sir Dennis moved into the house, for a while. He then sold it to William Hewer, who had been Samuel Pepys' clerk, and had risen to high office in the Civil Service. John Evelyn noted in *his* Diary, later: 'When King James the Second fled the Kingdom, Mr. Pepys laid down his office under Government, and would serve no more, but withdrawing himself from all public affairs, lived at Clapham with his partner, Mr. Hewer, formerly his Clerk . . .'

On 23 September, 1700, Evelyn wrote: 'Went to visit Mr. Pepys at Clapham where he has a noble and well-furnished house especially with India and Chinese curiosities the offices and gardens well accommodated for pleasure and retirement.' And on 26 May, 1703: 'This day died at Clapham Mr. Samuel Pepys a very worthy and industrious and curious person none in England exceeding him in knowledge of the Navy in which he had passed through all the most considerable offices, all of which he performed with great integrity.'

Gauden House—'a very noble and sweet place', commented Evelyn—had its principal front facing the Common and stood approximately where Victoria Road now runs. The estate was broken up and sold in lots in 1760.

On the other side of the Common, approximately at the corner of Cavendish Road, the world was first weighed, early in the eighteenth century. This unprecedented feat was carried out by Henry Cavendish, the famous philosopher and chemist, who was the eldest son of Lord Charles Cavendish who, in his turn, was the second son of William, the second Duke of Devonshire.

Almost the whole of Cavendish House, which was a large mansion in secluded park-like grounds, was used by Cavendish for his workshops. The room that had previously been used as the principal drawing-room was fitted up with thermometers, rain gauges, and other scientific instruments, and many of Cavendish's own inventions were distributed about it. In an adjacent room, there was a forge. The upper parts of the house were used as an astronomical observatory. Out on the lawn, there was an elaborate wooden staging from which access could be obtained to a large tree. On the top of this tree there was a platform that Cavendish could use for his meteorological, electrical and other researches.

Cavendish had an immense and very valuable library, but it was placed in the grounds at some distance from the house so that he should not be disturbed by anyone who might come to consult it. A few of his own particular friends were allowed to take books away, but no one, not even himself, was permitted to withdraw a book without giving a signed receipt for it. He was so absorbed in his studies that he resented any interruption. J. H. Michael Burgess, in his *Chronicles of Clapham*, published in 1929, tells an amusing story of an interview between the diligent scientist and a representative from his Bank: 'The Bankers with whom he kept his account, finding that his balance had accumulated to upwards of eighty thousand pounds, commissioned one of the partners to wait on Mr. Cavendish and ask what he wished done with it. On reaching Clapham and finding the house, the banker rang the bell, but had the greatest difficulty in obtaining admission. "You must wait", said the servant, "until my master rings his bell, and then I will let him know that you are here."

'In about a quarter of an hour the bell rang, and the fact of the banker's arrival was duly communicated to the abstracted chemist.

Mr. Cavendish in great agitation desired that the banker should be shown up, and as he entered the room, saluted him with a few words asking him the object of his visit. "Sir," replied the banker, "I thought it proper to wait on you as we have in hand a very large balance of yours, and we wished to have your instructions regarding it." "Oh! If it is any trouble to you, I will take it out of your hands. Do not come here to plague me about money." "It is not the least trouble to us, Sir," replied the banker, "but we thought you might like some of it turned to account and invested." "Well, well, what do you want me to do?" "Perhaps you would like forty thousand invested?" "Yes, do so if you like, but don't come here any more to trouble me, or I will remove my balance," replied the scientist.'

Cavendish who, in his cousin's words, 'buried his science and his wealth in solitude and insignificance at Clapham' left a million pounds, at his death, to be divided among his relatives.

Clapham reached its greatest period as a site for the homes of the wealthy and celebrated during the latter part of the eighteenth century, and the first decades of the nineteenth century. Among the place's most prestigious residents during that time were the banker named Henton Brown (who 'at his own great expense' planted the island in the Mount Pond with rare shrubs and trees and provided it with a pagoda-like summer house, fences and a bridge) and another banker, Henry Hoare, who, though he had great estates at Stourhead in Wiltshire and at Stourton Caudle in Dorset built himself an elegant villa, 'The Wilderness', by Clapham Common so that he could attend to his business in London 'without being obliged to sleep in its smoky atmosphere'.

Facing the Common, at the top of Battersea Rise, was a large house that Henry Thornton bought in 1792. It was of no great architectural merit, but it was designed for comfort, and so were the two rather similar houses, 'Glenelg' and 'Broomfield', that Thornton had built on the surrounding land soon after he bought it. Thornton and William Wilberforce lived together, as bachelors, in the original house for several years until Thornton married, whereupon Wilberforce moved into 'Broomfield'. These houses, then, were the headquarters of the Clapham Sect, the extraordinary body of late eighteenth- and early nineteenth-century Evangelists who caused almost as much excitement in religious circles as the Reformation itself. With Wilberforce as their very able spokesman in the House of Commons, these wealthy do-gooders managed to make the Slave Trade illegal, create the slave-free State of Sierra Leone, found the Bible Society and start the movement that has now become the Royal Society for the Prevention of Cruelty to Animals. Their pietistic and puritan sentiments coloured the whole of the Victorian era and influenced profoundly the lives of such powerful men as Gladstone.

Clapham, today, merges without any obvious dividing line into the neighbouring suburbs of Balham and Tooting. The Priory, at Balham, was the scene of the death of Charles Bravo, which caused one of the great mysteries of Victorian England.

On 18 April, 1876, Charles Bravo, a successful thirty-year-old barrister-at-law, returned to his comfortable home on the edge of Tooting Common and had dinner with the beautiful and wealthy young wife he had married only four months before, and with her companion, a Mrs. Cox. Before she agreed to marry Bravo, the lady had been, successively, the wife of Alexander Ricardo, Captain in the Grenadier Guards and a confirmed alcoholic, and, after Ricardo's death, the mistress of the celebrated Doctor Gully, lately of Malvern, who numbered among his patients such famous men as Thomas Carlyle, Charles Dickens, Disraeli and Alfred, Lord Tennyson. When she decided to marry for the second time, the future Mrs. Bravo promised never to see Doctor Gully again. 'It is the right thing to do in every respect,' she wrote to the man who was to be her new husband. Bravo, who had himself been closely involved with a woman at Maidenhead, appears to have agreed.

The meal enjoyed by the Bravos and Mrs. Cox consisted of whiting, roast lamb, and anchovy eggs on toast. Bravo drank Burgundy. Between them, the two women got through a whole bottle of sherry and the better part of a second bottle. At ten o'clock, Bravo was smitten with violent pains, and he started to vomit. He lingered on, in great physical distress, for three days. Then he died, having suggested to Mrs. Cox (or so she said) that he had taken poison deliberately.

A post-mortem examination was held on the following day at St. Thomas's Hospital. At this, signs of ulceration of the intestines were found in the deceased man, which suggested that he had died from the effects of an irritant poison. Next week, a coroner's inquest was held 'privately' at The Priory. The members of the jury were entertained with great cordiality, and at some expense, by Mrs. Bravo, and their verdict was that her husband had died from antimony poisoning. They were unable to suggest, however, how the poison came to be present in Bravo's body.

There followed some weeks of mounting excitement during which there were few people, fancying themselves as amateur detectives, who did not advance their own personal theories as to how Charles Bravo died. Some thought that Mrs. Bravo had poisoned him so that she might be free to continue once more her guilty association with Doctor Gully. Others thought that Mrs. Cox, fearing that she was to be dismissed from the Bravos' service at the husband's insistence, had taken some positive steps to protect her livelihood. Controversy raged more and more fiercely until, at last, the Lord Chief Justice felt himself compelled to quash the verdict of the original jury and to call another inquest. At this second inquiry, held in July 1876 at the Bedford Hotel, Balham, the miserable Doctor Gully, whom the wagging tongues had accused of complicity, was compelled to give evidence, but in spite of his, and all the other testimonies to which the members of the jury listened, they found that there was 'insufficient evidence to fix the guilt on any person or persons'. Florence Bravo herself died in Southsea only two years later, of alcoholism; Doctor Gully's professional career was ruined; Mrs. Cox left the country soon after the second inquest and went to live in Jamaica. The mystery is still unsolved and continues to fascinate amateur criminologists. The Bravos' house is now divided into flats.

CHAPTER ELEVEN

Wandsworth, Putney and Roehampton

DURING the Middle Ages, many important London business men chose to live up the Thames, at Wandsworth principally, so that they and their families would escape, as far as possible, from the plagues and fevers that made residence in the City almost intolerable.

By the time the Tudors occupied the throne, the ever-present threat of foreign invasion made it necessary for the authorities to set up 'butts' or shooting ranges in every substantial town and village so that the men of the place could practise archery. At Wandsworth, the butts were set up in 1581 and they were situated at the foot of West Hill. The people of Putney were slower at providing the prescribed amenities, and in 1595 the local authorities were fined 3s. 4d. for being without them.

On the summit of East Hill, in Wandsworth, now, there is a small railed burial ground where a stone records an invasion that really did happen, and which was entirely to change the character of the little residential town: 'Here rest many Huguenots who, on the revocation of the Edict of Nantes in 1685, left their native land for conscience sake, and found in Wandsworth freedom to worship God after their own manner. They established important industries, and added to the credit and prosperity of the town of their adoption.' The 'important industries' referred to on the stone included dyeing, and the making of hats. The Huguenot hatters brought with them the secret of making felt from hair and made great use of that of the rabbit. Hats made in Wandsworth, then, became so popular with the fashionable young men of the time that they were in great demand even in Paris.

The dyers' success was largely due, it seems, to the purity of the waters of the River Wandle, on the banks of which Wandsworth stands, and to the rare 'fixing' quality of Wandle water, which even today has not been fully explained. The Cardinals in Rome were glad to get their scarlet hats from Wandsworth. It was the only place, they said, where hats were made with dyes so fast that the colour could be guaranteed not to run in wet weather in bright red rivulets down the faces of the wearers.

By the latter part of the eighteenth century, the level ground by the Wandle was well supplied with industrial buildings. There were breweries and distilleries, a white lead manufactory, an iron foundry and snuff mills. There were cottages long afterwards known as 'Frying Pan Houses' where secretive Dutchmen produced brass skellets, kettles and frying pans without letting anyone know the methods by which their goods were made. Most important, perhaps, of all were the mills where 'bolting cloths' were woven. These were cloths without seams that could be used for separating fine flour from coarse flour. Benjamin Blackmore, a weaver of Exeter, discovered how to make them. He patented his method about the year 1783 so that nowhere else in the world but Wandsworth, where he set up his manufactory, could this be done.

Until quite late in Queen Victoria's reign, there were many roads in the Wandsworth and Putney district that were operated on the 'turnpike' system. In spite of the tolls people had to pay for using these roads, they were often in a very unsatisfactory state.

At the end of the eighteenth century, the tradesmen and manufacturers of Wandsworth who wished to transport their goods for export, but were handicapped by the condition of the roads between their town and the south coast, decided to make an iron railroad. It would go from Wandsworth to Croydon, they planned, and then via Reigate and Arundel to Portsmouth.

So, an Act of Parliament was passed in 1801, sanctioning the construction of the line, and allowing for the appointment of twenty-nine local directors. The Act also mentioned the construction of a basin or dock at the mouth of the Wandle. This was complete by January 1802. The line to Croydon, made of iron rails fixed to stone sleepers, was ready by July 1803. Before the opening ceremony, the line was tested with twelve wagons full of stones, each wagon weighing three tons. It was found that one horse could pull this weight at the rate of four miles per hour. At the formal opening, according to a contemporary report, the members of the committee 'went in waggons drawn by one horse, and to show how motion is facilitated by this contrivances a gentleman with two companions drove up the railway in a machine of his own invention at fifteen miles an hour'. The gentleman was probably Richard

Trevithick, and he was almost certainly driving the historic steam locomotive that he exhibited on a circular track by Gower Street, London, during the same year.

Putney, the suburb just to the west of Wandsworth, was called in Saxon and Norman times 'Putten Hythe' or 'Putta's Hythe', a 'hythe' being a landing place—probably one used by ferrymen stationed here for crossing the Thames. (The actual position of the 'hythe' is thought to have been at the end of Brew House Street, which is one of Putney's oldest lanes.)

During the Middle Ages, Putney was just a small village, with three great fields that were tilled in a three-year rotation: Thames Field, which lay between the settlement and the Beverley Brook, Park Field, which lay to the north of what is now the Upper Richmond Road, and Bason Field, which lay to the east of Putney Hill.

The place was first woken from its parochial calm during the Civil War. The first shock came in 1642, when the Earl of Essex, son of Queen Elizabeth I's old favourite and Captain General of the parliamentary forces, decided to bring his troops into Surrey, so that they should be more closely in touch with those of the king. To do this, Essex caused a bridge to be built on barges and lighters over the Thames between Fulham and Putney, and ordered that forts should be erected at each end, to guard it. (The fort on the Putney side of the river was not finally demolished until 1850.)

Then, in 1647, when King Charles I had been compelled by his captors to leave Newmarket and to move to Hampton Court, Oliver Cromwell, wanting to be as near as possible to the royal prisoner without being too far from Parliament, made Putney his headquarters for a period of three months, using the chancel of the local church as his council chamber and, it is alleged, transacting his business mainly round the Communion Table.

Once the advantages of having a bridge across the river at Putney had been seen, there were always a few local people in favour of a permanent structure being built. In April 1671 a Bill was actually introduced into Parliament for the purposes of promoting such an enterprise, but it aroused considerable opposition. Sir William Thompson, speaking for the forces of reaction, said: 'Mr. Speaker, London is circumscribed, I mean the City of London; there are walls, gates and boundaries the which no man can increase or extend. These limits were set by the wisdom of our ancestors, and God forbid they should ever be altered.'

Sir William went on to say that if the proposed bridge were built, 'quicksands and shelves would be created through the whole course of the river, barges would be high and dry at Teddington, and that not a ship would be able to get nearer to London than Woolwich'. The Lord Mayor of London's view was given by a Mr. Lowe. His Worship felt (said Mr. Lowe) that 'if carts went over Putney Bridge the City of London would be irretrievably ruined, and the many pieces of wood, thick and numerous as they must be, would stop the tide altogether'. The Bill was defeated by thirteen votes, and the project was allowed to drop for another fifty years.

Then, a petition signed by citizens living on both sides of the river who were tired of waiting for ferries was supported by the Prince of Wales (later, King George II) who found that he was inconvenienced, when he wished to go hunting at Sheen, by the lack of a bridge at Putney. At first, plans were made for a bridge of boats like that used by Essex's forces, but they were soon dropped in favour of the wooden structure proposed by Sir Jacob Ackworth. This cost nearly £24,000 to build, but by the time it had been open for two years it was producing an annual income of £1,500 through the imposition of tolls. The collection of these tolls was a very unpopular business. On one occasion, soon after the bridge was opened, the toll collectors were 'barbarously insulted', and after that alarm bells were hung on the toll houses so that assistance could be summoned in the event of attack.

Unlike Clapham Common and Tooting Common, which have suffered grievously from traffic pollution, Putney Heath has managed to retain a little of the rural quality which made it, for centuries, one of London's more favoured spots for political and private duels.

In 1652, for instance, George, Lord Chandos fought and killed Colonel Henry Compton on the heath. (Chandos was imprisoned and, in 1654, was tried with his second, Lord Arundel, and found guilty of manslaughter.) The Duke of York, second son of King George III, met Lieutenant Colonel Lennox on the heath in 1789, but the latter did not fire. Probably the most famous of all the encounters that have taken place at Putney was that between William Pitt, when he was Prime Minister, and a Mr. George Tierney, Member of Parliament. Mr. Tierney had given to some words of Mr. Pitt a meaning that was not intended, and the Prime Minister refused to accept an explanation. The two men met on the heath on a Sunday in May 1798. As both were ignorant of the use of firearms, they discharged their guns harmlessly into the air, a proceeding that is said to have given 'great satisfaction to the onlookers'. When Lord Castlereagh and Mr. Canning fought a duel on the heath in September 1809 one party, at least, was a little more efficient, for the latter was shot in the thigh.

William Pitt, as it turned out, was to spend his last days on Putney Heath. The great statesman had been, in very poor health, at Bath when Canning travelled down there to break to him the news of the disastrous defeat suffered by the Allied forces at the Battle of Austerlitz. On 9 January, 1806, Pitt, looking pale and emaciated, left Bath with Sir Walter Farquhar, his personal physician. On the 10th, the men halted at Reading, and on the following day they reached the Bowling Green House on Putney Heath (later known as 'Blenheim Lodge') where they were greeted by Lady Hester Stanhope. As Pitt entered the hall of the house, it was reported, he saw suspended on the wall a map of Europe. 'Roll up that map,' he is said to have exclaimed. 'It will not be wanted these ten years.' The bad news from the Continent may have hastened the great Tory's end, for he lingered less than a fortnight more, dying in the house on 23 January.

Near Bowling Green House, at that time, stood the Fireproof House, the scene of a strange experiment. The house had belonged to a Mr. David Hartly, a Member of Parliament, who had invented a plan for making buildings quite immune to the ravages of fire, and he had put his system into operation in his own place. In 1774 or 1776, King George III and Queen Charlotte drove over from Kew to inspect the house and were invited to sit down to breakfast in an upper room while the room below was turned into a mass of roaring flame. When the old mansion was renovated in 1814, the builders found that between each set of flooring planks, Hartly had had inserted sheets made of laminated copper and iron. These formed a crude 'safety lining' and helped to intercept the ascent of heated air. An obelisk was raised in the garden of the house to commemorate Hartly's unusual endeavours and it still stands, though the house itself is no more. (It was not burnt down, we hasten to say.)

Putney Heath was the scene, for many years, of the daily walk of a small, strange and very respectable figure who had been one of England's most considerable poets. When he lived at Tudor House, in Cheyne Walk, Chelsea, with Dante Gabriel Rossetti, Algernon Charles Swinburne's behaviour was wild and entirely unpredictable. He was frequently hilariously drunk; in warm weather he was apt to walk round the house stark-naked, which embarrassed the servants and surprised any guests who had not been previously warned what they might see; and he made stealthy visits to St. John's Wood, where he paid for the pleasures of flagellation. At last, in 1864, when neither Swinburne nor his share of the household expenses had been visible for months, Rossetti wrote his friend an 'affectionate and cordial' letter, in which he suggested that it might be better for both of them if Swinburne found somewhere else to live. After that Swinburne's decline was fairly rapid. By the time he was rescued in 1879 by the worthy Theodore Watts-Dunton and carried off to live at No. 2 The Pines, a prim semi-detached villa that still stands at the foot of Putney Hill, he was so dangerously low in health that he might well not have survived at all if the firm-minded solicitor had not taken him in hand and removed him to what was then an 'outer suburb' with strictly limited temptations.

The austere and regular life led at The Pines by the two men has been exactly chronicled, and much fun has been made of the single drink Watts-Dunton allowed Swinburne to take each day, on his solitary walks, at the pub by Putney Heath. It is not generally realised, however, how long this strange ménage was in existence. Swinburne, who was born in 1837, and who had shocked so many Victorians, died of pneumonia in 1909. Watts-Dunton survived for another five years.

It would be interesting to speculate on what Swinburne would have made of the entirely new London suburb that was put up on the western edge of Putney Heath just after the Second World War, and of the life style of some of its inhabitants.

At the beginning of the nineteenth century, there were only sixty-three houses, all told, in the charming little hamlet of Roehampton. When the London County Council acquired a large proportion of the ground in the area, with the intention of creating one of the largest planned housing estates in Europe, the land had on it only a few eighteenth-century mansions that had been built in the classical style as gentlemen's country houses (they still had extensive and beautifully timbered grounds) and a few quite ordinary middle-class suburban villas, with gardens, that had been built during the Victorian expansion of the capital. The mansions were preserved by the County Council's men; most of the nineteenth-century villas were demolished.

Into the informal, well-wooded site that remained, the local authority's architects put a number of lofty point blocks; high slab-like buildings standing on thin pole-like 'piloti' that were blatantly derived from Le Corbusier's *Unité* blocks at Berlin and Marseilles; long dreary four-storey blocks made up of shops and maisonettes; and two or three contemporary sculptures, including a chunky cast of Robert Clatworthy's 'Bull'. The architects thought that by preserving some expanses of grass and as many as possible of Roehampton's venerable trees, they would manage to keep the feeling of Roehampton's aristocratic eighteenth-century parkland. 'It was a new department at the L.C.C. with a lot of new blood', Bill Howell, one of the architects concerned, has recalled, 'and we were looking for a breakout from low-cost formula housing which was pretty depressing. We were looking for more variety, and mixed development did bring this.' It certainly did.

But there were difficulties with which the architects with new blood had not reckoned. They had intended that families, in their new estate, should stay on the ground, and that people without children should be up in the air. Somehow, things did not work out exactly according to plan. 'When Alton' [the name given to one part of the estate] 'was built, it was overpopulated with small children', commented another L.C.C. architect who worked with Bill Howell on the New Utopia. 'Then it was over-populated with teenagers—and that must be part of the problem, an overpopulation of teenagers in one of the largest housing estates in London. And I think you were creating a suburb, not a town.'

A psychiatrist working in a hospital close to the new estate was frankly critical: 'Mitcham, where I practise, is a very settled sort of place,' he told a leading newspaper after a sad incident yet to be described. 'It's an area with no large railway station, not much commuter population, not many boarding or lodging houses. It's very like the East End—the people who are born there grow up and die there; and it's an area from which we have almost no patients with gross psychopathic disturbances. The really unsettled people move out of places like Mitcham, because it's just boring.

'But Alton Estate is quite the opposite. It's impossible for people growing up there to become a member of the community. As they grow up, they know that whatever they do now has got nothing to do with their future life, and that must be unsettling in human terms.

'What they do isn't governed by a sense that they will be living next door to the people they encounter—they won't be marrying a girl whose father will be living nearby, for example, so the social constraints on violence are missing, in a place like Alton—because the social structure that provides such constraint is missing . . . There's no temporal community—no settled community in which there are all generations. You have cohorts of population at Alton, moving up together. From being an empty place full of people with no children, it becomes a place pullulating with kids and then full of teenagers looking for the action . . .' A new and potentially violent suburb had been brought, in one short decade, into being.

CHAPTER TWELVE

Mitcham, Merton, Wimbledon and Cheam

MITCHAM may be 'just boring', as the psychiatrist quoted at the end of the last chapter was blunt enough to suggest, but there are other places in the London Borough of Merton that are far from being dull.

Merton, the civic centre of the borough, lies eight miles from Westminster Bridge on the road that used to be the old 'turnpike' route to the South Coast. In the Middle Ages, the place was noted for its Priory, the religious house at which Thomas à Becket was educated, as well as Walter de Merton who, later, founded the Oxford college that bears his name. In 1536, King Henry VIII took possession of Merton Priory and had its buildings demolished. A few walls only have managed to survive.

Cheam, now a quiet suburb a little to the south of Merton, had its first brief period of national renown when it was chosen by the same King Henry VIII as the site for a new palace, not too far from London or from Hampton Court, from which he could hunt. Henry, who planned to put up a magnificent building that would far outshine all the fine palaces that were being built by his principal rival, François I of France, called the place, from the start, 'None-such', because it was to be, as we might say nowadays, 'the greatest'. With his customary ruthlessness, Henry served a compulsory purchase order on the manor, church and village of Cuddington, which happened to be standing on the spot he had chosen. He had them razed to the ground, and then he started to build his 'None-such', using in the foundations cartloads of stone from the old Merton Priory which he had just had pulled down.

The Palace was more or less completed by the time Henry died in 1547. His daughter Mary, who did not need or want a sumptuous hunting-box, gave it to Henry FitzAlan, twelfth Earl of Arundel, in exchange for four manors and a cash payment of £486 13s. 4d.

Then, Queen Elizabeth I took it back from Arundel's son-in-law, as settlement for a debt, and as it was a beautiful building, beautifully situated, it became one of her favourite homes. It remained a royal palace until 1649, when it was confiscated by the victorious Parliamentarians. At the Restoration, it was taken back into royal ownership again, but when King Charles II gave the place (probably riddled with woodworm and dry rot after all those years of neglect) to his mistress Barbara Villiers, Countess of Castlemaine, she sold it, as potential building materials, in a desperate attempt to pay off her debts. So, None-such was demolished forthwith, and even the exact site of the building was uncertain until archaeological excavations were carried out in 1959–60. (Three stones in Nonsuch Park, now, mark the spot.) There are several walls in Merton, today, that are believed to have been built with None-such bricks.

The most distinguished residents of Merton in recent centuries have been, without much doubt, Admiral Lord Nelson and Emma, Lady Hamilton. The house at Merton, which Nelson was determined to buy, though the price asked was really beyond his means, was described by the surveyor he sent to look at it, a Mr. Cockerell, as: 'An old paltry small dwelling of low stories and very slightly built, at each end of which has been added (very unsubstantially) a very gross room, and nearly the whole of the body has been rendered weak for communication to them. The Offices behind are even worse than the House and the roof and other parts are so much out of repair that before they can be furnished and comfortably inhabited at least £1000 must be laid out.'

The house itself stood on only an acre and a half of ground, Mr. Cockerell pointed out, and was liable to be annoyed by the meanest buildings or other nuisances that might be placed close to it. Its straightened boundary was circumscribed by a 'dirty black-looking canal, or rather a broad ditch', which kept the whole place damp. It was, the surveyor concluded, 'altogether the worst place under all its circumstances that I ever saw pretending to suit a Gentleman's family'.

In spite of the local expert's gloomy warnings, Admiral Lord Nelson was determined to have the 'dear farm'. Two days after he received Mr. Cockerell's unfavourable report, he wrote to a Mr. Haslewood, who was handling the property and who, disliking Lady Hamilton, preferred to deal with Lord Nelson direct: 'I would have the place bought, as good a bargain as can be made. Your friend Mr. Cockerell is not a Judge of what may suit my fortune.' To underline his interest in the place, Nelson insisted on buying at valuation all the furniture which Mr. Cockerell had described as being 'so inferior that it must (also) be replaced with new'. Probably, Nelson was desperately anxious at that time to have a place in which he and Emma might be able to behave a little more like the master and mistress of the house, and where Sir William Hamilton, Emma's lawful but ageing husband, with whom they had been living, might be demoted diplomatically to the rank and status of an honoured guest. Where, in short, the nation's hero and his beloved Emma might have a chance of being more often left alone together, when Nelson was ashore.

Once the house was safely bought, Emma could hardly get into it quick enough. 'Curse the Lawyers, I hate them all!' she wrote bitterly when the vendor, an old woman called Mrs. Greaves, refused to vacate the place before the agreed date. 'The Lawyers are a lot of villans or it might have been finished ten days past. Yesterday I send Dods [Nelson's banker's man] to beg her to give it up as Milord [Nelson] was expected and could not sleep in town. She had the impudence to say "Well. Let Milord come down with one servant and stay with us till the thing is finished, we will make it comfortable to him." What do you think, my dearest friend, of her *impudence*! What would Nelson say was I to tell him of it—"She be d—" you know the rest. A likely story, *he* would go down with one servant and stay *with her*! My patience is gone and my head not the better for it . . .'

Once Mrs. Greaves had been paid and had departed, Lady Hamilton, accompanied by her husband, took possession and quite fell in love with the place. 'A seaman alone could have given a fine woman full power to chuse and fit up a residence for him without seeing it himself', wrote Sir William to the absent Admiral. 'You are in luck, for in my conscience I verily believe that a place so suitable to your views could not have been found, and at so cheap a rate, for if you stay away three days longer I do not think you can have any wish but you will find it compleated here, and then the bargain was fortunately struck three days before an idea of peace got abroad. Now every estate in this neighbourhood has increased in value, and you might get a thousand pounds tomorrow for your bargain. The proximity to the capital, and the perfect retirement of this place, are, for your Lordship, two points beyond estimation; but the house is so comfortable, the furniture clean and good, and I never saw so many conveniences united in so small a compass. You have nothing but to come and enjoy immediately; you have a good mile of pleasant dry walk around your own farm. It would make you laugh to see Emma and her mother fitting up pig-sties and hen-coops, and already the Canal is enlivened with ducks, and the cock is strutting with his hens about the walks. Your Lordship's plan as to stocking the Canal with fish is exactly mine. I will answer for it, that in a few months you may command a good dish of fish at a moment's warning . . .'

The interior of the 'earthly paradise' Lord Nelson and Emma had found at Merton was soon fitted up, like a shrine, to the glorification of its new and illustrious owner. 'I went to Lord Nelson's on Saturday to dinner,' wrote Lord Minton, 'and returned today in the forenoon. The whole establishment and way of life is such as to make me angry as well as melancholy . . . She looks ultimately to the chance of marriage, as Sir William will not be long in her way, and she probably indulges a hope that she may survive Lady Nelson; in the meanwhile she and Sir William and the whole set of them are living with him at his expence. She is in high looks, but more immense than ever. She goes on cramming Nelson with trowelfuls of flattery, which he goes on taking as quietly as a child does pap. The love she makes to him is not only ridiculous, but disgusting; not only the rooms, but the whole house, staircase and all, are covered with nothing but pictures of her and him, of all sizes and sorts, and representations of his naval actions, coats of arms, pieces of plate in his honour, the flagstaff of *L'Orient* &c.—an excess of vanity, which counteracts its own purpose. If it was Lady Hamilton's house there might be a pretence for it; to make his own a mere looking-glass to view himself all day is bad taste . . .'

On 2 November, 1805, the *Morning Post* reported that there was a rumour that there had been a naval engagement off Cadiz. Emma, at Merton, was understandably nearly distraught with anxiety. Four days later, the news reached London that there really had been a battle, that the British fleet had been victorious, and that Admiral Lord Nelson had been fatally injured on his flagship the *Victory*. The tidings were taken to the lady waiting at Merton in Admiral Collingwood's words: 'I have not only to lament, in common with the British Navy and the British Nation, in the fall of the Commander in Chief, the loss of a hero whose name will be immortal, and his memory ever dear to his Country; but my heart is rent with the most poignant grief for the death of a friend . . .'

Emma, grievously stricken, took to her bed at the farm for a time, leaving it only to be removed from Merton to her bed in her 'small house' in Clarges Street, Mayfair. Her heart was broken, she wrote from there. Life to her was not, thereafter, to be worth having, since she had lived only for her 'glorious and dear departed Nelson'. Her health and spirits were so bad that she could not even enter into a war with the 'vile editor' who had published four of the last letters that Nelson had written to her.

Emma's associations with Merton, after that, were bedevilled by her financial embarrassments. She had been left the house and part of the land, it is true, but she had to find the money, somehow, to pay for the improvements Nelson had commissioned, and she was quite incapable of living frugally. The house was put on the market in April 1808 but it did not change hands until April 1809 when it was bought by a friendly banker named Goldsmid. The new owner of the farm did not have time to get much pleasure from his purchase, for, fearing that his own finances were in serious disarray, he committed suicide in the following year.

Now, almost all the local evidence of Lord Nelson's stay at Merton has disappeared, for the house he lived in with Emma was demolished in 1840, and the canal has been filled in. His hatchments still hang in the Parish Church, though, and there is a house in the High Street at Wimbledon, not far away, that he used to visit. This quietly handsome mansion, now called 'Eagle House', was built by Robert Bell, an original member of the East India Company, in 1613. In the eighteenth century it was the home, successively, of the Marquis of Bath, Sir William Draper (the man who defended Lord Granby against the lashings of 'Junius') and Lord Grenville, who was Speaker of the House of Commons and a relative of William Pitt. In the early nineteenth century the Reverend Thomas Lancaster, Vicar of Merton, made the house into a school, which he named 'Nelson House' in honour of his distinguished parishioner. The house was given its modern name by a Doctor Huntingford who took over the school in 1860 and installed the stone eagle—brought from his previous school building in Hammersmith—in its present proud position on the gable.

'The Guide Books do not exaggerate when they claim that Wimbledon is the most beautiful, dignified, and refreshing of all suburbs which adjoin the greatest capital city in the world . . . In it, men and women may live near the enjoyment of almost complete rural scenery and yet be within eight miles of Leicester Square.' Those words, written by Guy Boas, who was one of Wimbledon's most devoted historians, are still to a certain extent true, though Boas has been dead for some years. It is still possible to stand in the High Street and to imagine, as groups of young girls clad in jodhpurs or breeches chatter past on their way to or from riding, that one is actually in the country, or very near it. Even the dogs to be seen in Upper Wimbledon tend to be of the beagle or hunt terrier type, rather than of some more urban breed.

Most of the rural atmosphere of Wimbledon is due, of course, to the presence of Wimbledon Common, that carefully preserved mixture of woodland and open ground which extends over hundreds of acres. In the heart of the Common, there is even a windmill, that dates from the year 1817. (It was rebuilt, to a certain extent, in 1890.) Here, during the early years of this century, Baden-Powell wrote part of his classic *Scouting For Boys*.

The ground near the Windmill, like that near the lake known as 'Queensmere' and a stretch of the Heath near the 'Green Man' at Putney, was a favourite location for duels, and the last of these battles-of-honour to be fought (as far as is known) on Wimbledon Common did actually take place by the mill.

The duel, on 12 September, 1840, was provoked by a letter signed 'H.T.' which had appeared in the *Morning Chronicle*, and which purported to give a true account of the action of the seventh Earl of Cardigan (later, to be the leader of the Charge of the Light Brigade at Balaclava) in ordering the arrest of an officer named Captain Reynolds. The writer of the letter, one Captain James Harvey Tuckett, and the disgruntled Earl of Cardigan met, with pistols, at five o'clock in the afternoon and shots were exchanged, Captain Tuckett being severely wounded by a bullet which entered his body below the ribs.

On the following Monday, James Thomas, seventh Earl of Cardigan, aged forty-two, and John Douglas, Captain in the 11th Hussars, who had been his second, appeared before two magistrates at Wandsworth, charged with 'wounding with intent to murder'. The magistrates tried to send the case for trial at the

Central Criminal Court but the Earl of Cardigan claimed his right to be tried, instead, by his Peers. The case, heard on 16 February, 1841, lasted only one day, being brought summarily to an end when the Court decided that it had not been proved that the 'Captain Tuckett' mentioned in the indictment was one and the same person as the Captain Harvey James Tuckett who had acted so painfully as a target for His Lordship up on Wimbledon Common. At that, the Peers present declared with evident relief that Cardigan was 'Not Guilty upon my Honour', and the Earl was discharged.

In the same year there died, in Wimbledon, the 'Duchess of Cannizaro': a woman—according to Charles Greville, who rarely missed an interesting bit of scandal—whom the world laughed with and laughed at while she was alive, and would 'regret a little because she contributed to their entertainment'. As Cannizaro House, rebuilt since then and made into an Old Folks' Home, is still one of Wimbledon's most notable buildings, this seems the right place for the romantic story behind its unusual name.

The house that stood originally on the site belonged, until 1748, to Thomas Walker, who amassed a mighty fortune as King George I's Commissioner of the Customs and who was, besides (in Horace Walpole's words), 'a great frequenter of Newmarket and a notorious usurer'. Under the terms of Walker's will, the house and the surrounding estate passed into the hands of the Grosvenor family and it remained Grosvenor property until the present century.

During the intervening years, the place was leased by the Grosvenors to a succession of extremely wealthy and extremely unusual people. Lyde Brown, Governor of the Bank of England, had it for a number of years and he used it to house his famous collection of Greek and Roman works of art. (In 1787 he sold the cream of this collection to the Empress Catherine of Russia for £22,000.) Henry Dundas, First Viscount Melville, took it after that, and entertained William Pitt there frequently, but Dundas decided in 1805, after he had successfully but expensively defended himself against England's last impeachment, that he could no longer afford to keep up so vast a mansion, and he was forced to move out to a smaller house by Wimbledon Common, naming his new home 'Duneira Cottage' after one of his Scottish estates.

Soon after Dundas moved out, the Johnstones, brother and

sister, moved in. Miss Johnstone was the daughter of Commodore George Johnstone, Governor of West Florida, and a director of the East India Company. According to Greville, the heiress was 'very short and fat, with rather a handsome face, totally uneducated, but full of humour, vivacity, and natural drollery, at the same time passionate and capricious'. Her all-absorbing interest was music, and nearly all of her time and much of her wealth was devoted to the pursuit of her hobby. Shortly after the death of her brother, the now immensely wealthy Miss Johnstone married a good-looking, intelligent but penniless Sicilian nobleman: Francis Platemone, Count St. Antonio, afterwards, 'Duke of Cannizaro'. The Count soon became disgusted with his rich English wife and went back to Italy, living on a separate allowance that she provided for him. After a few years he returned to England and they tried living together again. But, says Greville:

> He not only became more disgusted than before, but he had in the meantime formed a liaison at Milan with a very distinguished woman there, once a magnificent beauty, but now as old and as large as his own wife, and to her he was very anxious to return. This was Madame Visconti (mother of the notorious Princess Belgioso), who, though no longer young, had fine remains of good looks, and was eminently pleasing and attractive. Accordingly, St. Antonio took occasion to elope (by himself) from some party of pleasure at which he was present with his spouse, and when she found that he had gone off without notice or warning she first fell into violent fits of grief, which were rather ludicrous than affecting, and then set off in pursuit of her faithless lord. She got to Dover, where the sight of the rolling billows terrified her so much, that, after three days of doubt whether she should cross the water or not, she resolved to return and weep away her vexation in London. Not long afterwards, however, she plucked up courage, and taking advantage of a smooth sea she ventured over the Straits and set off for Milan, if not to recover her fugitive better half, at all events to terrify her rival and disturb her joys. The advent of the Cannizaro woman was to the Visconti like the irruption of the Huns of old. She fled to a villa near Milan, which she proceeded to garrison and fortify, but finding that the other was not provided with any implements for a siege, and did not stir from Milan, she ventured to return

to the city, and for some time these ancient heroines drove about the town glaring defiance and hate at each other, which was the whole amount of the hostilities that took place between them . . .

Finding that her husband was irrecoverable, the stout old Duchess at length got tired of the hopeless pursuit and decided to return to Wimbledon. With her, she took a fiddler from a second-rate theatre in Milan, and with this fellow she had a singular and curious affair. 'There was not the slightest attempt to conceal their connexion', Greville recorded. 'On the contrary it was most ostentatiously exhibited to the world, but the world agreed to treat it as a joke, and to do nothing but laugh at it.' Unfortunately for the Duchess, the Italian fiddler turned out to be a blackguard who bullied and robbed her without mercy or shame, and by the time she died her immense fortune had dwindled quite away. What little she had left, she bequeathed to her absentee husband, in spite of his infidelities.

In May 1859, the Volunteer Force was founded, which was later to become better known as the 'Territorial Army'. Two months after that, a few of the officials of the movement, including Earl Spencer, decided to form a 'National Rifle Association'. These worthy gentlemen, nostalgically aware of the days of the Plantagenets when archery was the principal pastime of the English people, and when English archers were the terrors of England's foes, aimed to promote rifle shooting in place of archery through the length and breadth of the British Isles. 'Competition', said Lord Elcho in a letter to *The Times*, 'is the life and soul of our national sports. How long would cricket flourish without "Lord's", or horse-racing without "The Derby"? We want then to encourage Volunteers and rifle shooting in Great Britain by establishing an annual "Rifle Derby".'

Many places were considered for the first meeting of the new Association, but finally Wimbledon Common was selected as having 'a picturesqueness of its own as well as the necessary space and accessibility from London'. Earl Spencer, as Lord of the Manor, had offered to place his Common at the disposal of the Association, but his action aroused the fury of many of the less influential residents of the place when they found out what their Feudal Master had been up to.

The second day of July 1860 was chosen as the opening date of the first great Wimbledon meeting, and Queen Victoria, approached by Earl Spencer, agreed to attend and to fire the first shot. From then on, though, it seemed as if the elements were determined to prevent the great Save Britain meeting from taking place at all, for rain poured down consistently day after day for weeks and the officials of the Association were driven to almost endless unforeseen expenditure as they tried to drain the sodden ground and make it a little less like a waterlogged swamp.

In spite of the appalling weather, the Queen and the Prince Consort managed to reach the Common at the appointed hour. After loyal addresses had been presented to them, the royal party proceeded to a specially built pavilion, where the rifle with which Her Majesty was to fire the inaugural shot had been fixed in a mechanical rest. A silken cord attached to the trigger was handed to the Queen by a Mr. Whitworth, who had made the necessary adjustments to the rifle. 'The rifle having been fired by a sharp pull', recorded the official chronicler, 'it was found that so accurately had the rifle been adjusted that the bullet had struck the target within a quarter of an inch of the centre.'

The first meeting of the Association saw only a few official tents and refreshment booths pitched on the Common. The event was so successful, though, that in the following year the assembly round the ranges looked more like a well-attended regimental camp. A review of ten thousand Volunteers was organised, to conclude this second meeting, and a 'mock battle' was arranged the year after that. (Anticipating, it is believed, the yearly spectacles known now as the 'Royal Tournament'.)

From then on, the annual shooting matches on Wimbledon Common were among the most important events in the British social calendar. Long lines of carriages streamed dutifully out from the capital each summer so that their fashionably dressed occupants could struggle up the hill to Wimbledon and share 'the charm of the wide Surrey moorland and the free open air life of the Volunteer'. (The words are taken from a Souvenir Handbook, prepared in 1910, the Jubilee Year of the meeting.) At one of the early meetings, Jenny Lind, the 'Swedish Nightingale', who was then living in Wimbledon, gave a special recital in one of the official tents. Sir Edwin Landseer, the famous Royal Academician, designed an artistic 'Running Deer' moving target for the Association, and G. F. Watts, R.A., dutifully followed Landseer's illustrious example by designing an alternative target known as the 'Running Man'. Huge quantities of liquid refreshments were consumed in the evenings, and thousands of delightful 'al fresco' meals were eaten, under canvas or outside, according to the weather. But the 'Last Post' was sounded sternly in the encampments at half past ten, and after that visiting relatives and others were sent away and silence was strictly enforced. Shooting, and the probable defence of England, was too serious a business to be interfered with by headaches and hangovers.

It was all too good to continue indefinitely. The local inhabitants were enraged by Earl Spencer's well-meaning attempts to close the Association's camps on Sundays, when there was no shooting—he only wanted to keep out 'undesirables', who might thieve, but the Wimbledonians were not prepared to treat the matter as simply as that—and they continued to grumble on about the annual invasion of 'their' Common until 1887, when the steadily increasing population of the hilltop village and the steadily increasing danger to life and limb caused by stray bullets persuaded the officials of the Association to find a new site for their annual jamborees. Bisley, in outer Surrey, was settled on, and the 1889 meeting of the Association was the last to be held on Wimbledon Common.

Just before the rifle shooters moved away from Wimbledon, another sport took root in the district which was to make the name of the place famous all over the world.

The All England Club was born, really, on 24 July, 1868, when a sports writer named Henry Jones, his cousin Whitmore Jones and two other croquet enthusiasts met in the office of J. W. Walsh, editor of *The Field*, to explore the possibility of starting a croquet club. Between them, the men managed to raise five pounds to finance the search for a suitable ground.

The search went on for more than a year. The Crystal Palace authorities at Sydenham were approached, but the proprietors of the great showplace of the age expressed no interest. Nor did the managers of the Princes Club in Hans Place, Knightsbridge. In Regent's Park, the Royal Toxophilites did not like the the suggestion that their archery might be diluted with a little croquet. Six acres were available in Holland Park, but the rent was £500 per annum, so the five-man committee turned down this offer with regret.

At Wimbledon, there was a site of four acres just off Worple Road, and adjacent to the London and South Western Railway.

The rent was £50 per year, but it was due to be doubled. The five men raised £600 between them, signed an agreement, and arranged that the ground should be laid out at a cost of £425. By the end of 1869 a pavilion had been built, and the All England Croquet Club was officially, and tangibly, in existence. In 1870 a croquet championship was staged at the ground.

While this search for suitable premises for croquet had been going on, a new game—'lawn tennis'—which had been evolving for some years from an ancient game of 'real tennis', 'royal tennis' or 'court tennis', had become sufficiently popular for some official recognition to be sought for it. On a lawn in Edgbaston, near Birmingham, in 1868, a Major Gem and a Mr. Perera had marked out a court. In 1870 the game was played in Leamington on the lawns of the Manor House Hotel. (A plaque there, today, records that 'on this lawn in 1872 the first lawn tennis club in the world was founded.)

The Marylebone Cricket Club, offered the use of the name 'Lawn Tennis' by one of Queen Victoria's Honourable Gentlemen-at-Arms, a Major Walter Clopton Wingfield, who regarded himself as the original inventor, called a meeting to discuss the new game and to formulate its rules. At this point, or soon after, the M.C.C. offered the game to the Croquet Club at Wimbledon because women wanted to play it, and they knew the club at Worple Road had female members. Henry Jones, who was always a keen innovator, supported the M.C.C.'s suggestion and proposed that part of the Wimbledon grounds should be devoted to the new-fangled game. £25 was allocated for the necessary equipment. At first tennis was only allowed on certain days of the week. But it soon became popular.

By 1877 the All England Club was running out of money. One of the Club's most urgent needs was to repair a wide roller, designed to be drawn by a horse or pony, that had been given to the Club in 1869 by a Mr. J. W. Walsh, for nothing, on the understanding that his daughter would be made an honorary life member. At a committee meeting held in the Spring of 1877, Mr. Walsh proposed that to defray the cost of repairing the roller, a Lawn Tennis Championship should be held, open to all comers. His fellow committee members agreed, and Mr. Walsh persuaded the proprietors of *The Field* to present a silver challenge cup worth twenty-five guineas.

There were twenty-two entries for the first Lawn Tennis Championship to be held at Wimbledon. The winner was an Old Harrovian named Spencer Gore. Gore was a devotee of rackets and 'real' tennis, but in spite of his success—now seen to be historic—he failed to work up any enthusiasm for the new sport. In 1890 he wrote: 'It is its want of variety that will prevent lawn tennis in its present form from taking rank among our great games. . . . That anyone who has played really well at cricket, tennis or even rackets will ever seriously give his attention to lawn tennis, beyond showing himself to be a promising player, is extremely doubtful: for in all probability the monotony of the game as compared with the others would choke him off before he had time to excel in it . . .'

The winner of the All England Club's second Tennis Championship, held in 1878, P. F. Hadow, also an Old Harrovian, was on leave from the coffee plantations of Ceylon. He was even cooler than Spencer Gore had been. Having won the championship, he returned to Ceylon, never played lawn tennis again, and never even saw a first class tennis match until 1926, when he was invited back to Wimbledon for the Jubilee celebrations of the club.

In spite of the *sang froid* of Gore and Hadow, the tennis side of the Worple Road club increased in popularity so tremendously that its name soon had to be changed to the 'All England Croquet and Lawn Tennis Club', and then, a little after that, to the 'All England Lawn Tennis and Croquet Club'. The person who put Lawn Tennis resoundingly on the international scene, however, was, without any doubt, the French girl, Suzanne Lenglen.

Lenglen was a prodigy, and she was a perfectionist, and she was a crowd-puller. Before she was fifteen, in 1914, she had won the Hard Court Championship of the World. She was dramatic in everything she did, and always had to be the centre of attention, even when she was carrying out such a commonplace action as entering a room. Her virtuosity attracted so many spectators (and, therefore, so much money in admission fees) to Wimbledon that shortly after the First World War the All England Club was encouraged to move to larger premises.

In 1922 the Championships were held for the first time at the Club's present grounds in Church Road. Instead of having a maximum viewing capacity of about seven thousand, as at the old ground, the new Centre Court alone could seat over ten thousand people, in addition to providing an unprecedented amount of standing room. (At Worple Road, the Centre Court had really been at the centre of the layout. At Church Road, it is well to one side, but the old name was, and is, attached to it.)

Ironically, it was on the new Centre Court in 1926, the Jubilee Year of the Club, that Suzanne Lenglen made her dramatic, and famous, non-appearance. For years, it had been the custom for an official of the Club to escort Mlle. Lenglen to the referee's office at the close of each day's play, so that she might be informed of the time that she would be required to turn up on the following day. For some little time, though, there had been an undoubted clash of temperaments between the formidable Frenchwoman and the equally formidable referee F. R. Burrow. On the evening before the day in question, no one was asked to call for Mlle. Lenglen, and she left Wimbledon in a state of some dudgeon, believing that she would only be required to play in a women's doubles match at half past four on the following afternoon.

Later in the same evening, however, Mr. Burrow decided that Mlle. Lenglen should play a second round ladies' singles match at 2.30 p.m., *before* she played in the women's doubles at 4.30 p.m. The Royal Family were told, and Queen Mary, who was also a quite formidable figure, said that she would have an early lunch so that she could get to Wimbledon in time to see Mlle. Lenglen play in her singles match. Nobody told Mlle. Lenglen.

At 3.30 p.m., then, the great Frenchwoman arrived at Wimbledon thinking that she had a clear hour in hand in which to prepare for her doubles match. To her horror, she was summoned at once to appear before the Committee, the members of which were appalled by the insult that had apparently been offered to Her Majesty the Queen, and severely reprimanded. Mlle. Lenglen then slammed off to the Ladies' dressing-rooms and went into a violent fit of hysterics. Soon, it became obvious that the transcendental star of tennis would be in no proper state, for emotional reasons, to play a single game that day. By the end of the week, the hostile publicity she had received and the critical reception she had been given by the Wimbledon crowd in subsequent games had clearly been too much for Mlle. Lenglen to stand, and she withdrew first from the singles championship and then from the tournament altogether. She never played amateur lawn tennis again, preferring to turn professional.

Wimbledon now gets an enormous amount of international

publicity for staging what a present-day commentator, John McPhee, has described as 'the world's most glittering tourney in any sport', but this quiet suburb hits the headlines, occasionally, for other and less creditable reasons.

On 18 August, 1969, for instance, shortly before midnight, a young police constable named Davies, who had just played a leading part in a film made for and about the Metropolitan Police, went for a stroll across Wimbledon Common with two of the local rangers and their wives. When the party reached Queensmere Lake—'recognized', Counsel said later, 'as an international haunt for homosexuals'—P.C. Davies was stabbed fatally by a man who was afterwards committed to Broadmoor after the prosecution had accepted his plea of 'Guilty' to manslaughter, on the grounds of diminished responsibility.

Five weeks later, a twenty-eight-year-old solicitors' clerk, Michael De Gruchy, was battered to death with boots and sticks on the edge of Wimbledon Common by a group of young men who had wandered over from their homes on the nearby Alton Estate looking, as was said earlier, 'for the action'.

Then, as if to round off a terrible year for Wimbledon, December 1969 saw the beginning of the 'Mrs. McKay Case'. The middle-aged wife of the Deputy Chairman of the *News of the World* group of newspapers was kidnapped from her home in comfortable Arthur Road. Demands for large sums of money followed, and a heart-rending note, written on cheap blue air mail paper, was received: 'Alick darling, I am blindfolded and cold. Please do something and get me home. Please co-operate or I cannot keep going. I think of you all constantly and have kept calm so far. What have I done to deserve this treatment?'

In spite of all the tremendous efforts made by the police and 'all men of goodwill', no part of Mrs. McKay was ever found. Two brothers named Hosein were sentenced to long terms of imprisonment, though, for the part they were alleged to have played in her disappearance.

CHAPTER THIRTEEN

Richmond, Mortlake and East Sheen

THE eminent nineteenth-century novelist Mary Russell Mitford once wrote to a friend of hers: 'Richmond is Nature in a court dress, but still Nature—aye, and very lovely nature too, gay and happy and elegant as one of Charles the Second's beauties, and with as little to remind one of the penalty of labour, or poverty, or grief, or crime. To the casual visitor (at least) Richmond appears as a sort of fairyland, a piece of old Arcadia, a holiday spot for ladies and gentlemen, where they have a happy out-of-door life, like the gay folks in Watteau's pictures, and have nothing to do with the workaday world.'

There are plenty of gay folks in Richmond's 'sort of fairyland' today, though they may not be exactly the type of person envisaged by Mary Russell Mitford in all her monumental Victorian innocence. In general, though, Miss Mitford's view of Richmond as a happy holiday spot has still a certain amount of truth today. It is certainly one of the most elegant and Arcadian of all London's suburbs, even if it is no longer entirely free from labour, or poverty, or grief, or crime.

There may have been a manor house on this lovely stretch of the Thames as early as 1066. The first manor here of which there is any positive record belonged to King Henry I (1100–35). This would have been a typical country house of the period, with a large central hall and with a few rooms leading from it. The place was then called 'Shene' or 'Schene'.

By the reign of King Henry III (1216–72) the Court had taken to visiting Shene fairly frequently, and a number of houses had been built round the manor to accommodate the courtiers and members of the royal household. King Edward I and his Queen Eleanor of Castile stayed at the enlarged royal settlement fairly often and Edward received the Scottish Commissioners here in 1300. When they visited the manor there was usually a tourney held on the large field in front of the manor house. (We know it today as 'Richmond Green'.) To watch the competing knights, the king and queen would sit on a gorgeously draped platform outside the gates of their country home.

Edward II had little chance to relax at Shene—he had too many wars and rebellions to keep him busy—but Edward III did die in the place, in 1377, after doing much rebuilding and enlarging. Richard II's first wife Anne, daughter of the Emperor Charles IV, was particularly fond of Shene, and practically made it her home.

Then came disaster. In 1394, when the plague was raging in London, many people fled the city, and some of them made their way to Shene. It is possible that Queen Anne caught the infection from one of these refugees, for she was taken ill at Whitsuntide and died within a matter of hours. At first Richard could not grasp the fact that Anne was dead, as she was the only human being for whom he had genuinely and passionately cared. When at last he was persuaded that she would never come back to him, he became half crazed with grief and rage. His anger turned itself on the place where he and Anne had known so much happiness and he cursed Shene, every stick and stone of it, and gave orders that the manor house should be pulled down. Almost immediately after the Queen's funeral procession left for London, workmen started to carry out the King's punitive instructions.

It was left to King Henry IV to build Shene up again, but in 1499 the royal riverside residence was once more the scene of disaster. As Francis Bacon recorded in his *Life of King Henry VII*: 'A great fire in the night-time suddenly began . . . near unto the King's own lodgings, whereby a great part of the building was consumed, with much costly household stuff . . .' The fire burned fiercely for over three hours, spoiling the manor that the Queen and her children dearly loved (they liked it so much more than the other royal homes at Eltham, Greenwich and Windsor) and destroying most of its contents. Like a good husband and father, Henry undertook to rebuild the house yet once more. Once he had had a chance to talk over possible plans with the master craftsmen who would be responsible for its construction and furnishing, he started to think in larger terms. As Bacon put it: 'He builded it up again sumptuously and costly, and changed the name of Shene, and called it Richmond, because his father and hee were Earls of Rychemonde [the town in Yorkshire] . . .'

The area in the immediate neighbourhood of the rebuilt royal home was called, from that time on, 'Richmond', or some variation on the word, the name 'Shene' being kept for the east and west parts of the ancient manorial lands.

The house, itself, was much more like a palace than the old manor had been. The complex of brick and timber buildings, which contained a Great Hall one hundred feet long and forty feet wide, a chapel hung with cloth of gold, and many other expensively furnished apartments, covered an expanse of nearly ten acres, commanding the whole of the river front from what is now Old Palace Lane to Water Lane. The royal lodging, a freestone building three storeys high, with fourteen lead-covered turrets, was said to be 'a very gracious ornament to the whole house and perspicuous to the country around'. The closeness of Richmond Hill, which is well supplied with natural springs, made the provision of running water for the palace relatively easy, and there was an elaborate stone fountain in one of the courts: 'Ornamented with lions and red dragons and other goodly beasts, and in the midst certain branches of red roses, out of which flowers and roses is evermore running a course of clear and most purest water into the cistern beneath. This conduit profitably serves the chambers with water for the hands, and all other offices as they need to resort . . .'

Early in November 1501, according to a manuscript written by Lancaster Herald, which is still preserved in the College of Arms, King Henry invited his new daughter-in-law, Princess Catherine of Aragon, to spend a week-end in the newly refurbished Palace of Richmond. With the Princess, came her Spanish entourage. As the water gate at Richmond was still at that time unfinished, the party had to disembark from their barges in the late evening in the nearby village of Mortlake (or Mortlak, Mortelac, Moortlack, Mooreclacke, Mortelak, Mourtlake, Mortelage, Murtelac, More Clack, Mortylack, Mortelake—it was spelled at the time in various ways). They rode on, then, by torchlight to Richmond.

Catherine's husband, Prince Henry, was also fond of Richmond, and when he became king in 1509 he started to stage elaborate tourneys on the Green, and engaged distinguished companies of players to perform masques for the entertainment of the Court. When he took a fancy to Thomas Wolsey's grand new home upstream at Hampton, however (the Cardinal's place was much more spacious than the one at Richmond, and thought to be more distinguished, architecturally) and when Wolsey thought it politic to offer Hampton Court to the King, Henry, in return, invited the Cardinal to live in the Palace he was vacating. Wolsey accepted the King's generous offer, but he was not to be allowed to use Richmond for long. He soon fell from grace, and was stripped of his treasures. When that happened, the once-proud man went to live in a lodge in what is now the Old Deer Park. It was part of the old Monastery of Shene, and there the Fathers of the House 'persuaded him from the vain glory of this world, and gave him divers shirts of hair, the which he often wore after'. Then, Henry settled the Manor on Anne of Cleves.

When Henry's daughter Queen Elizabeth I took up residence at Richmond, and she was as fond of the place as her grandfather and grandmother had been, she found herself drawn, as if by a magnet, to the quiet downstream village of Mortlake, for there, in a rambling old house that stood just to the west of the church, lived an extraordinary man. He was the son of Rowland Dee, who had been Gentleman Server to Her Majesty's father.

This person—commemorated, now, by a block of council-owned flats called 'John Dee House' in Mortlake High Street—was primarily a mathematician and an astrologer, but he was also a distinguished cartographer, so that many of the leading navigators of the time such as Frobisher, the Gilberts and Hawkins, journeyed up-river from London to see him before they set out on their voyages of exploration and discovery. All Dee's visitors were impressed by their host's belief that he would eventually be able to realise the alchemist's age-old dream and discover how to change base metals into gold.

On her first visit to Dee's house, the Queen went purposely with her lords and privy councillors to see the great scholar's library. When she arrived, however, she found that his wife had died, and had been buried in the churchyard only four hours before. She said that she would not go into the house, therefore, but she asked Dee to fetch his famous 'seeing glass' or crystal, and there, by the churchyard wall, the bereaved man gave the Queen a demonstration of its remarkable qualities.

Dee, after that, was highly regarded in royal circles. When her courtiers, in 1577, were greatly alarmed by the appearance of a comet, the Queen sent for him to go to Windsor so that she could listen to his explanations of the heavenly phenomenon. (Dee talked for nearly three days.) About the same time, his services were urgently called for when a wax image of the Queen was discovered in Lincoln's Inn Fields with a pin stuck through its breast. (Dee was required to forestall any harm that might accrue to his royal patron from this alarming discovery.) Then, in 1582, when Pope Gregory proposed that changes should be made in the Calendar, it was Dee who had to make the calculations that were necessary before the new Calendar could be adopted in England.

About this time, Dee came under the malign influence of a rogue called Edward Kelly, alias Talbot, who hailed from Worcestershire. Kelly, who was twenty-eight years younger than Dee, had already been convicted of forgery and had lost his ears in the pillory at Lancaster. To hide his mutilations, he constantly wore a black skull cap, with flaps, which, it is said, made him look very wise and scholarly. Kelly called on Dee one day and said he wished to see or show something 'in spiritual practice'. Quite taken in by Kelly's blarneying tongue and oracular appearance, Dee showed the stranger his 'seeing glass' and described the spirits that seemed to be 'answerable'. After the two men, at Kelly's suggestion, had joined in prayers and exhortations, a spirit called Uriel manifested itself in the Mortlake room (or, at least, Kelly told Dee that Uriel had appeared). Uriel, through Kelly, then gave directions for invoking other spirits and insisted that Dee and Kelly should, from then on, co-operate in their researches. So, Kelly was installed as Dee's official seer, or 'skryer', with an annual salary of £50, and he remained in the post for more than a quarter of a century. Dee appears to have believed implicitly in the 'revelations' made by Kelly, and whenever Kelly threatened to leave he would be ready to make almost any offer to retain his services. The good people of Mortlake did not think much of him, though, and when the two 'magicians', to restore their flagging fortunes, set off on a Continental tour at Kelly's suggestion, the villagers broke into Dee's house and smashed the place up.

Mortlake attracted royal attention again in James I's reign, when the king granted an annual subsidy to a Sir Francis Crane, who wished to establish a 'woven pictorial tapestry workshop' on the side of the late lamented Doctor Dee's laboratory on the north side of the High Street.

The factory started well. Fifty Flemish weavers were given employment; a man called Francis Klein from Rostock was appointed to supervise the designs; and Mortlake tapestries were soon greatly in demand and commanded high prices. (Some were even exported to various parts of Europe.) In 1635, however, the proprietor died, and in the following year the workpeople were forced to take a petition to King Charles I in a desperate attempt to obtain the wages that they said were owing to them. The King did intervene, but the rot had set in. The factory was finally finished off by the Civil War, for it was then seized by the Parliamentary authorities and handed over to the care of John Holliburie, the foreman or 'master workman', who allowed the whole enterprise to fail. (One must not be hard on him: the times were out of joint.)

The most significant change made by King Charles I in the Richmond area was, of course, the enclosure of some 2,500 acres to make a new hunting preserve. Richmond Park is, today, one of Southern England's finest nature reserves, with large herds of deer and a splendid collection of English trees, many of which were growing in their present situations even before the ground was enclosed.

The King's great project was opposed, from the start, by some of the local landowners whose property he needed to take. (A few agreed to settle at once for the very fair prices His Majesty offered them.) More serious opposition came from Thomas Laud, Bishop of London, and Lord Cottington, who was the King's Chancellor of the Exchequer. Laud was against the King's scheme because he knew that by pressing ahead Charles would make himself even more unpopular with the citizens of London than he was already. Cottington was against it because the enormous cost of purchasing so much land, and of building round it so long a brick wall (almost ten miles of it, according to one estimate) would put an intolerable strain on the national finances. Charles, obstinately, started to build the enclosing wall on those parts of the ground that were already his, and as the park grew, the local opposition began to crumble away as the land-users began to realise that they would have to come to terms or risk being cut off, arbitrarily, by the Monarch's personal preserves.

The end of the Civil War brought great changes to Richmond, and to the new Park, as it did to most of the rest of the country. The Royal Palace, valued at over £10,000, was sold to Thomas Rookesby, William Goodwin, and Adam Baynes. They re-sold it to Sir Gregory Norton, one of the judges who had signed the death warrant of the King. He died, little more than a year later, and the place sank into a state of neglect. King Charles II looked at it after the Restoration, but as he much preferred Windsor he offered it to his mother as her home. Henrietta Maria, used to the luxuries of the White House at Greenwich, found it bleak and lacking in comfort without its former splendid furnishings. So, the Old Palace was largely dismantled. Only the Gate House, in which Queen Elizabeth I is believed to have lain, in a stricken state, during her last illness, and the Wardrobe were left standing. These fine medieval buildings confer extraordinary distinction on a quiet corner of Richmond today.

Richmond Park was given by the Parliamentarians to the Citizens of London, but the Citizens of London gave it back, at the Restoration, in an access of joy at the downfall of the Puritans, to the Crown. From then on, it was enjoyed hugely by most of the occupants of the throne, King William III and Queen Mary being particularly fond of hunting there.

In the early eighteenth century, Richmond came to be regarded as a particularly attractive place in which gentlefolk from London could settle, or where they could have their second homes. So, gracious and elegant Queen Anne and early Georgian houses can be seen there in great variety.

There was no longer a residence in the town suitable for Royalty, though, and this state of affairs went on until 1724, when King George I's son, the Prince of Wales, bought for £6,000 an old mansion called 'Ormonde Lodge' which stood in what is now the Old Deer Park. The Prince and his wife detested the Prince's autocratic old father the King, and at their new home, which was called from then on 'Richmond Lodge', they set up a minor Court of their own. Unfortunately, however, the accommodation at Richmond Lodge proved to be much too limited for such metropolitan goings-on, so the Prince promptly ordered that four new houses should be built by the old Gate House overlooking the Green, for the Princess's Maids of Honour. The exteriors of these splendid houses are almost identical. All have five tall sash windows, surmounted by ornamental keystones, on the first floor, and each has a forecourt enclosed by wrought iron railings, with an ornamental gate.

Charles Dickens may have had Maids of Honour Row in mind when he wrote in *Great Expectations*: 'We came to Richmond all too soon and our destination there was a house by the Green: a staid old house, where hoops and powder and patches, embroidered coats, rolled stockings, ruffles, and swords, had had their court days many a time. Some ancient trees before the house were still cut into fashions as formal and unnatural as the hoops and wigs and stiff skirts; but their own allotted places in the great procession of the dead were not far off, and they would soon drop into them and go the silent way of the rest.'

In June 1727, King George I died, when he was back in his native Hanover on a visit. As soon as the news reached London, Sir Robert Walpole, the Chief Minister of State, called for his horse and galloped from his Chelsea home along the country roads to carry the tidings to the new King at Richmond Lodge. George II did not at first properly appreciate Sir Robert, and contemptuously dismissed him from office, appointing in his place Sir Spencer Compton, a 'plodding, heavy fellow, with great application but no talents, his only pleasures, eating and drinking'. Within a very few months, Sir Robert had been re-instated and—this was important for Richmond—he, or rather his eldest son Lord Orford, was given the Rangership of the Park. (Unofficially, father and son seem to have shared the pleasures and responsibilities of this particular job).

Spurred on by the new King, who was a great sportsman, Sir Robert and his son set about draining the Park. Before their arrival it had been boggy, and a haunt of deer poachers and worthless men, but they started to convert it into a beautiful and well-stocked hunting ground. To please the King, they were asked to install flocks of wild turkeys in the Park. (The wretched birds, chased by dogs, were forced to fly up into the trees, so that His Majesty could shoot them without difficulty or fatigue.) In August 1728, in the *Stamford Mercury*, there appeared this agreeable news item:

> On Saturday their Majesties together with their Royal Highnesses the Duke (of Cumberland) and the Princesses, came to the new park by Richmond from Hampton Court and diverted themselves with hunting a stag, which ran from eleven to one, when he took to the great pond, where he defended himself for half an hour, when he was killed. His Majesty, the Duke, and the Princess Royal hunted on horseback, her Majesty and the Princess Amelia in a four-wheeled chaise, and the Princesses Mary and Louisa in a coach. Her Majesty was pleased to show

great condescension and complaisance to the country people by conversing with them and ordering them money. Several of the nobility attended, amongst them Sir Robert Walpole, clothed in green as Ranger. When the diversion was over, their Majesties, the Duke, and the Princesses refreshed themselves on the spot with a cold collation, as did the nobility at some distance of time after, and soon after two in the afternoon returned to Hampton Court.

Soon after that, the King and his family did not have to return to Hampton Court or anywhere else after a morning's hunting, for the sporting monarch had commissioned Lord Pembroke to design for him a 'shooting box' in this quiet rural retreat, and the construction of the main block of it was already quite well advanced. (The house, built of Portland stone, was referred to, at first, as 'The Stone Lodge'. Then, to distinguish it from 'The Old Lodge', which was Walpole's house in the Park, it became 'The New Lodge'. It was given, finally, the name by which we know it today —'The White Lodge'.)

Walpole spent many hundreds of pounds of his own money improving The Old Lodge for his own use and enjoyment, and before he (or his son) had been Ranger for long he had got into the habit of spending practically all his week-ends there, insisting that he could do much more work in the quiet of the country than he could in the bustle of Town. (According to the *Dictionary of National Biography*, the closing of the House of Commons on Saturdays dates from this period.)

On two occasions at least the Prime Minister had to be fetched urgently from Richmond Park when Queen Caroline wished to see him at short notice. On the first occasion, in 1736, the Queen wanted to tell the Prime Minister that the King, who was on his way to visit one of his current mistresses in Germany, had safely reached Helvoetsluys in Holland. Obviously resenting Walpole's absence from the capital, the Queen asked Lord Hervey to summon him at once. Lord Hervey, according to his *Memoirs*, promptly dispatched a messenger to Sir Robert at The Old Lodge, letting him have the good tidings about the King's safety, but not venturing 'to tell him that he found the Queen looked upon his retirement with Miss Skerrett to Richmond Park just at this juncture as a piece of gallantry which, considering the anxiety in which he left Her Majesty, might have been spared, as well as the gallantry of His Majesty's journey to Hanover which had occasioned that anxiety . . .'

Towards the end of Sir Robert's time as Ranger, or co-Ranger, the question of public access to the Park became more than usually vexed. Sir Robert felt that the amount of money that he had spent on 'improvements', and the special cares of his high office, entitled him to complete privacy and freedom from casual intruders. So, he had the old 'ladder-stile' gates removed from the walls for by these, the Park could be entered at almost any point on its perimeter. Then, to control entry to the Park more effectively, he had small lodges built at the official gates, and in these buildings he installed keepers who were ordered to admit 'respectable persons' in the daytime, and those carriages, only, to which special brass passes had been issued. The local people protested vociferously at this arbitrary curtailment of their privileges, but the Walpoles stood firm, and the locals, gentry and bumpkins alike, grumbled in vain.

Tension mounted further in 1751, when the Princess Amelia, the King's youngest daughter, took over the Rangership of the Park, the Earl of Orford having died. The Princess made The White Lodge her principal home and treated the Park entirely as if it were her private property, closing it to the public altogether, and admitting only her own personal friends and a few other persons to whom she granted special permits. The locals, seething with rage, tried to remind the Princess that free access had, traditionally, been allowed to the Park ever since the land had been enclosed by King Charles I. The Princess did not even bother to reply.

The first real skirmish in the great Who-Owns-The-Park struggle came three years later, when a number of gentlemen led by a Mr. Symons tried to enter the Park but were refused permission by one of the gatekeepers, whose name was Deborah Burgess. The gentlemen then brought a legal action against the Deputy Ranger, one James Shaw, more than £1000 being subscribed by the residents of East Sheen to meet the expenses of the case. The trial, conducted by the Lord Chief Justice, lasted two days, but after a number of witnesses called by the defence had testified that anyone prepared to pay 2s. 6d. (then, quite a large sum) could enter the Park, the verdict went against the plaintiffs.

But one stout-hearted Richmond man refused to accept the

validity of this judgment. This was John Lewis, a brewer, who was determined to carry on the fight, if necessary, alone, to get the townspeople's ancient rights of access to the Park restored. Gilbert Wakefield, brother of the Vicar of Richmond, recorded the story as he heard it from Lewis: 'Lewis takes a friend with him to the spot [East Sheen Gate]; waits for the opportunity of a carriage passing through; and when the doorkeeper was shutting the gates, interposed and offered to go in. "Where's your ticket?" "What occasion for a ticket: anybody may pass through here." "No; not without a ticket." "Yes, they may, and I will." "You shan't." "I will." The woman pusht, Lewis suffered the door to be shut on him, and brought his action . . .'

Lewis's suit—brought, in the first instance, against the 'doorkeeper', the burly Deborah Burgess—was really aimed against the Ranger, the Princess Amelia, and everyone knew it. For three years the Crown managed to prevent the case from being brought into court, but at last, through Lewis's quiet persistence, it was heard at Kingston Assizes on 3 April, 1758.

The trial, held before Sir Michael Foster, of the King's Bench, lasted a day. Lewis did not press for unrestricted entry to the Park for both pedestrians and vehicles as he had seen from the previous case that this argument would be unlikely to succeed. Instead, he based his case on the rights of way granted by King Charles I to those on foot. The verdict was given in Lewis's favour, and there were loud cheers in court.

The Judge then asked the plaintiff if he would prefer a door to be made in the wall of the Park, or a step-ladder set up, by which it might be climbed over. Lewis, realising that a gate would have to be kept shut to prevent the deer escaping from the Park, and that it would probably be kept bolted, too, told the Judge that he would choose the step-ladder.

Within a month of the Assizes, ladder-stiles fitted with gates had been built, like bridges, over the Park walls near East Sheen and Ham, and a 'vast concourse of people from all the neighbouring villages' assembled and attempted to climb over into the Park.

But they had under-estimated the resourcefulness of the Princess Amelia. Incensed by the decision of the court that had been given against her, the Royal Park Ranger had given instructions that the rungs on the ladder-stiles should be spaced so far apart that they would be almost impossible to use.

Once again, John Lewis took the matter to court. When he told Mr. Justice Foster that old men and children would be quite incapable of negotiating the Princess's ladders, he found the Learned Judge, once again, entirely sympathetic to his cause. 'I have observed it myself', said His Worship. 'And I desire Mr. Lewis, that you would see it so constructed that not only children and old men, but old women, too, may be able to get up.'

John Lewis became a popular hero in the locality, after that. (When his printing business ran into difficulties, as a result of a great flood tide that swamped his premises, the townspeople of Richmond clubbed together and gave him an annuity.) The Princess Amelia, quite disgusted, resigned the Rangership of the Park and went off to live over the river, at Gunnersbury.

The White Lodge did not remain empty for long after the Princess's abrupt departure. From 1801 until 1844, it was occupied by Viscount Sidmouth (better known, perhaps, as 'Henry Addington'). Many famous men were entertained at The White Lodge during Lord Sidmouth's time, the most distinguished of all, perhaps, being Admiral Lord Nelson who went there for dinner just five weeks before the Battle of Trafalgar and is said to have traced out on a table, with wine, the scheme with which he intended to destroy his opponent's lines should he ever be lucky enough to encounter the enemy fleet.

After Lord Sidmouth's death in 1844, The White Lodge became once more, for more than a century, a Royal Home. Queen Victoria's aunt, the Duchess of Gloucester, lived in it for a time while she was ostensibly acting as Park Ranger. In 1858, Edward, Prince of Wales, was put in the Lodge with his tutors. Three years later, Queen Victoria herself moved into the place, after her mother had died and she wanted some peace and quiet in which to recover from the shock. When the Queen no longer wanted it any more, she handed it on to her relations, the Duke and Duchess of Teck, who took a great interest in local affairs, and were very much liked.

While the Tecks with their daughter Mary—a future Queen of England—were in residence on the high ground, one of the country's greatest travellers and most extraordinary characters, Sir Richard Burton, K.C.M.G., F.R.G.S. etc., was interred down in Mortlake's quiet little Roman Catholic cemetery, just to the north of the Southern Railway Company's busy commuter line which, just then, was causing much of the ground between the river and the Park to be built over with rather monotonous houses.

Burton was the author of more than fifty books, and translator into English of the fabulous stories of the beautiful Scheherezade (*The Tales of the Arabian Nights*). He first achieved fame in 1853 when he made an unprecedented pilgrimage to Mecca, the city that was then strictly forbidden to all non-Moslems. To get there without being recognised and promptly put to death, he passed himself off as an Indian pathan, and he did this successfully enough to account for any peculiarities or defects that might be noticed in his speech. He was awarded the Gold Medal of the Royal Geographical Society after that, for an even more hazardous journey he made to explore the interior of the Somali country in North-East Africa. In 1856, he made one of his greatest expeditions of all, when he attempted vainly to establish the source of the Nile.

Burton's fame, or what is left of it, is equalled now by that of his dynamic wife Isabel, who, during his lifetime, tried vainly to convert him officially to Roman Catholicism, her own faith. Burton, a mixture of agnostic, Theist, and oriental mystic, firmly refused to do what his wife wanted. It was only when he lay dying and helpless in Trieste in 1890, that the ruthless Lady Isabel got her way. Then, she sent urgently for a Catholic priest. The priest—a Slav peasant from a nearby mountain village—arrived just after Burton had expired, and, knowing that Burton had never declared himself a Catholic, refused to administer Extreme Unction. 'I besought him not to lose a moment . . . for the soul was passing away', wrote Lady Isabel, later, recalling her anguish on that ghastly occasion. In one of the most commanding of all Victorian female voices, she argued that her husband had for a long time been a Catholic 'in private', that his body was not yet cold, and that his pulse might yet be beating faintly, if only one could feel it. Convinced of the eternal justice of her cause, Lady Isabel remained prostrate and in tears on the floor and, in a state of near-hysteria, refused point blank to listen to reason. At last the poor priest weakened, and probably to save the desperate woman from further agony, consented to administer the sacraments *Si Vivis* or *Si Es Capax* to the wholly uncomprehending explorer.

The members of Burton's own family—staid Anglicans, to a man and woman—were appalled. They regarded Lady Isabel's action as a kind of spiritual kidnapping. Appalled, too, were those stern Protestants who believed that proselytising, by Catholics, was one of the greatest crimes of the age.

Undaunted, Lady Isabel returned to London, while Burton, in his coffin, was sent home by sea. Despite ill-health she travelled up to Liverpool to meet the boat and forgot the spectators, herself, and everything else when she saw the coffin again, embracing it with heart-rending sobs. Meanwhile, the authorities at Westminster Abbey had been unaccountably cool to Lady Isabel's suggestion that they might like to have her husband's body buried there; nor had the authorities of St. Paul's Cathedral deigned to offer him a place. Thoroughly disgruntled, Lady Isabel declared that a grave in the Abbey would have been altogether unworthy of her beloved husband, anyway, since there he would have had to share the attention of geographically-minded pilgrims with such minor explorers as Livingstone and Speke. She would do better for him, she said. She would build a great mausoleum specially for her hero in the little Mortlake graveyard in which so many members of her family were buried. And, it would be a really remarkable one, worthy of her husband's extraordinary qualities. 'I don't want to burn before my time,' he had once said to her, when they had been discussing cremation, 'but would like to lie in an Arab tent.' Lady Isabel remembered this. An Arab tent, then, it would be.

So, after public subscriptions had been invited, to help to defray the cost, huge blocks of Carrara marble were soon being moved with the greatest difficulty into the quiet little suburban burying ground and stone masons started to chip merrily away. Before long, the astonished Mortlakians saw behind their Catholic church, the stony representation of a Bedouin tent. The tent-effigy, fringed and gilded, had, at each end, a golden nine-pointed star that looked for all the world, to the irreverent, like a lightning conductor. Across the door there was stretched a rope hung with camel bells that swung and tinkled in the smallest breeze. Lady Isabel was delighted. Her life would only be complete, she declared, when she could join her husband in 'the most beautiful, the most undeathlike resting-place in the wide world . . . An Eastern tent *above* ground'. Meanwhile, she decided, he was to have 'love, tears, prayers and companionship even in the grave', and, in a characteristic resolve to see that he was not allowed to lie quietly and in peace during the rest of her lifetime she rented a small house by the cemetery so that she could take tea each day, with her friends, within earshot of the tomb. (Unkind critics suggested that Lady Isabel used to pour out refreshments *inside* the tent, but no positive evidence of this has ever been adduced.) The Burton mausoleum still stands at Mortlake today, though nowadays it looks, like some of the streets around, a little jaded and in need of a face-lift.

The people who live in the suburbs round Richmond Park today are extraordinarily fortunate. Through the six carriage entrance gates round the Park's perimeter—at Richmond, Kingston, Ham, East Sheen, Roehampton, and at Robin Hood Gate on the Kingston By-pass—or through the five foot gates—the Bishop's Gate, the Bog Gate, the Cambrian Gate, the Ladderstile Gate and the Petersham Gate—they can enter, without payment, an enchanting area in which wild life is most carefully preserved. In 1937, C. L. Collenette, who was at that time the Park's official bird observer, recorded no fewer than 132 different species, of which forty-six were residents, that is birds which would normally breed in the Park, and some of which would stay there through all the different seasons of the year. By 1970, the number of different species of birds seen had shrunk to a hundred. Some may have left because they did not like the great tower-like blocks of flats that were by that time overlooking parts of the ground, but as recent stayers and visitors have included three kinds of Grebe, Tree-creepers, Goldfinches, Redchats, Stonechats, Black Redstarts and a single Singing Tree Pipit, keen ornithologists still have plenty to go for. The Park also contains some delightful plantations, one of the most generally admired (The 'Isabella') containing an extraordinary collection of flowering shrubs, such as Rhododendrons, Azaleas, Camellias, with Magnolias, and Heathers, and a running brook, artificially diverted, that is edged with waterside plants of innumerable kinds. If only King Charles I could see what he began!

CHAPTER FOURTEEN

Twickenham and Kew

As early as A.D. 704, the riverside land at Twickenham must have had its own special identity, for the same 'Tuicanham' can be seen in a charter prepared in that year and preserved, now, in the British Museum. Around the year 1230, a great park was carved out from the waste lands that lay on the bank of the Thames between the tiny settlements at Twickenham and at Isleworth, a little way upstream. The park was given permanent shape by being enclosed with the traditional hedge and ditch, except where the river itself acted as a boundary. This piece of marked-off land remained as one single unit until the beginning of the nineteenth century. It was given various names but here, for the sake of simplicity, it will be referred to just as 'Twickenham Park'.

In 1408, Pope Gregory XIII officially relieved King Henry IV of England of blame for the murders of King Richard II and Archbishop Scrope. But, there was a catch. In return for this generous judgment Henry had to undertake to found and endow three new religious communities. It was a form of penance. And rather expensive.

The work was actually done by Henry's son King Henry V, who, on his accession in 1413, inherited all his father's debts and obligations. The younger Henry decided to place the three monasteries within easy reach of the old Royal Manor of Shene, which he was determined to rebuild. An ideal site for one of the monasteries lay just over the river from Shene, namely Twickenham Park, which had been given by Parliament to Isabella, the beautiful but ruthless widow of King Edward II, but which had been taken back from her, three years later, by her son Edward III, and, since then, had remained in the hands of the Crown. The Park, said Henry, would do splendidly as a level and spacious setting for the monastery, to be used partly, by the monks of the Order of St. Augustine and partly by the ladies of the newly established Order of St. Bridget.

9a. William Morris. Painting by G. F. Watts

A. C. Swinburne. Chalk drawing by R. P. Staples

9c. Samuel Smiles. Pencil Drawing by Louise Jopling-Rowe

10a. Lord Nelson's Villa at Merton, 1806. Engraving by Warren

10b. Mill on Wimbledon Common. Engraving by George Cooke

11a. Richmond Lodge, in the Old Deer Park

11b. Maids of Honour Row, Richmond Green

12a. View of Kew, showing George II leaving Kew escorted by the Life Guards

12b. Marble Hill House

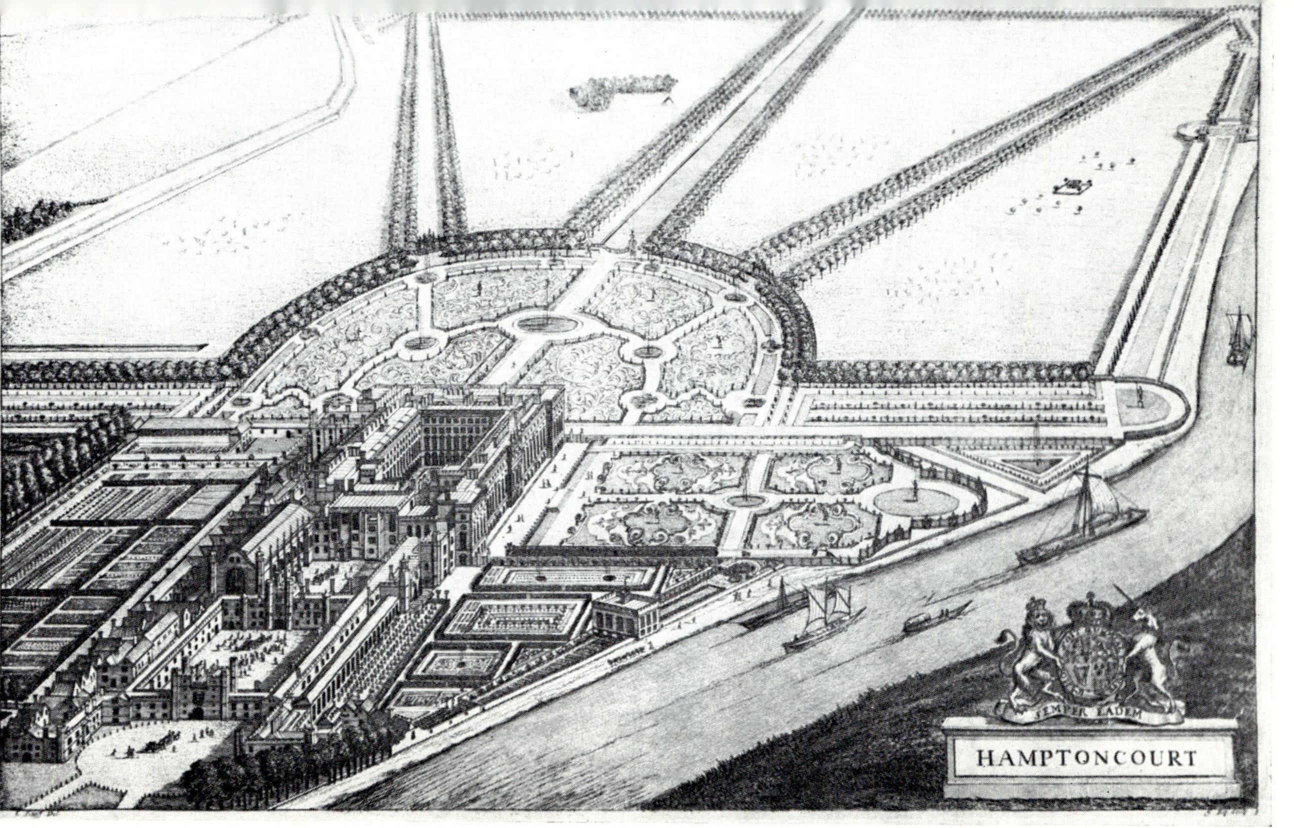

13. Hampton Court. Engraved by J. Kip. c. 1707

14a. Chiswick House, showing the Serpentine River

14b. Chiswick Mall in 1820

15a. William Kent.
Painting by B. Dandridge

John Zoffany. Self Portrait of the artist in 1761

16a. Brentford High Street, c. 1900

16b. Bedford Park Estate, Turnham Green, 1877

Henry had decided that the new monastery in Twickenham Park should be called 'Syon'.

So, on 22 February, 1415 the young king crossed the river and laid the first stone of his proposed monastery in the presence of Richard Clifford, Bishop of London. Nine days later, Henry signed a Royal Charter that would 'Found, ordain and for ever establish a certain monastery of the Order of St. Augustine called St. Saviour . . . And we will and decree that it shall be called "The Monastery of St. Saviour and St. Bridget of Syon" through all successive ages.'

The members of the foundation were bidden 'to celebrate divine service daily for ever for our healthful estate while we live and for our soul when we shall have departed this life, and for the souls of our most dear lord and father, Henry, late King of England, and Mary his wife, our most dear mother . . . And of other our progenitors and of all the faithful departed.' The buildings were to consist of 'a certain monastery, together with the church, cemetery, bell-tower, bell, houses, habitations, beds, bedding, gardens, courtyards, plots and other utensils and offices necessary for the habitation of the Father and seventeen Brothers and eight Conversi [lay brothers] . . . Also another monastery adjoining the same . . . But separate and entirely distinct from it, for the habitation of the Mother and Nuns and lay sisters numbering sixty persons . . .'

In spite of all Henry's lofty words and pious intentions, the site chosen for the new monastery appears to have been damp and unhealthy. The industrious monks dug a great ditch or canal, over three hundred yards long, in an effort to drain the land and make it more suitable for human habitation, but the Abbess and her nuns decided that they would like to move to a drier spot a few hundred yards away. In 1431, then, King Henry VI formally gave them permission to move to a site they liked much better, and on which they had already started to build.

The new and greatly enlarged monastery stood, more or less exactly where the Duke of Northumberland's great mansion ('Sion House') stands today. Being a royal foundation, the monastery was unusually well-endowed and enviably well-equipped. It had one of the largest and finest libraries in the country, and one of its greatest treasures, the famous and beautifully embroidered Sion Cape, is now one of the most revered exhibits in the Victoria and Albert Museum.

The site that the religious folk had vacated was much too good to be allowed to revert to pasture, so on it a great mansion was built, probably incorporating the deserted monastic buildings and enhanced, certainly, by the monks' long drainage canal which became, after that, an invaluable decorative feature (and still is, today). The house stood just inside the corner formed where St. George's Road, Twickenham and The Avenue now meet.

In 1574, Queen Elizabeth I made over Twickenham Park on a twenty-one year lease to her 'dear well-beloved subject' Edward Bacon, third son of the Lord Keeper of the Great Seal. The Queen charged her tenant only four pounds and ten shillings yearly, as he would be acting as Keeper of the Park. Francis Bacon, Lord Chancellor of England, stayed at the Park during long periods of his life since he found the quietness and isolation of the place particularly suitable for study and contemplation. He took refuge from the Plague there in 1592. Later in the same year, the Queen went to visit him: 'About the middle of the Michaelmas Term [he wrote] Her Majesty had a purpose to dine at my Lodge at Twickenham Park, at which time I had, though I profess not to be a poet, prepared a sonnet directly tending and alluding to draw on Her Majesty's reconcilement to my Lord Essex . . .' Three years later, the Queen granted Bacon a reversionary lease of the whole of the Twickenham Park estate. He kept the place until 1606 when, having got himself almost hopelessly into debt, he was compelled to sell the lease and move out.

The next important tenant of the Park was Lucy, Countess of Bedford. The Countess was a distant cousin of King James I for they were both descended from the ancient Bruce family. Having been invited to act as Lady-in-Waiting to King James I's daughter the Princess Elizabeth, Lucy Bedford looked round for a suitable home that would not be too far from Kew, the quiet Thames-side village into which the Princess had recently moved. Asked, in 1608, if she would be interested in taking over the lease of Twickenham Park, the Countess accepted at once, and proceeded to set up there a household 'maintained on so generous a footing that it seemed a small repetition of Lady Elizabeth's establishment and was even compared to it'.

From that time until 1619, when the Queen died, Lady Bedford took a leading part in all the festivities and amusements of the Court. Though she had other residences, including Bedford

House in Covent Garden, it was at Twickenham Park that she sought 'a happy relief from the distractions and intrigues of Court', entertaining there such great literary figures as John Donne, on whom she rained 'sweet showers of gold', and Ben Jonson, to whom she gave great haunches of venison carved from the deer that wandered over her estate. Her immense fortune was all too easily dissipated, and when the Countess died in 1627, a few days after her husband, she had, it was recorded, 'no belongings'.

The big house at Kew, usually known as 'The White House' or 'The Old Palace', originally belonged to Richard Bennet, son of Sir Thomas Bennet. His daughter married Lord Capel, who lived there until he died in 1696 and who, from his interest in strange and exotic plants, can really be regarded as the founder of the present Kew Gardens.

John Evelyn, on 24 March, 1688, recorded in his *Diary*: 'After dinner we went (from Sheene) to Kew, to visit Sir Henry Capel's, whose orangery and myrtetum are most beautiful, and perfectly well kept. He was contriving very high palisadoes of reeds to shade his oranges during the summer, and painting those reeds in oil . . .'

Lady Capel went on living in the house until she died in 1721. About nine years later, the property was leased from the Capel family by Frederick, Prince of Wales, the eldest son of King George II. Prince Frederick was a difficult and rebellious young man who was constantly quarrelling with his parents. When his own first child was born—at St. James's Palace, as Frederick wished, instead of at Hampton Court, as the King insisted—the row was so heated that Frederick was ordered to move out of St. James's and to take his family with him. Having, as Prince of Wales, an income of his own, he was able to take a town house in Leicester Fields and, as his country residence, the Capels' place at Kew.

With the arrival of royalty, the White House had to be enlarged and redecorated, so the celebrated architect and 'man of taste' William Kent was called in to do this, and to 'landscape' the gardens as well. Before long, all the most promising of the young gentlemen and the prettiest and liveliest of the young ladies had drifted quietly away from the Court that revolved round the King and Queen and were to be found, instead, in or around the elegant 'palace' at Kew.

But the Prince of Wales was not to enjoy the Crown, after all. He died quite unexpectedly in 1751, leaving a large family. The Princess of Wales, who had become so suddenly the Dowager Princess, decided to stay on at Kew, and to devote herself to training her eldest son, George Frederick, who had become, on his father's death, the heir to the throne.

In 1757, the members of the House of Commons gave leave for a bill to be brought in, which would allow the building of a bridge across the Thames from Old Brentford, in the parish of Ealing, to the opposite shore. The leave was granted in consequence of a petition from a Mr. Tunstal, the owner of the Kew ferry, who proposed to build the bridge himself, provided a reasonable toll should be granted him by way of compensation. There was a great deal of opposition from the occupiers of the nearby houses, who thought that Kew Green, on which they had been accustomed to pasturing 'all manner of Cattle', would have its herbage unnecessarily destroyed by passing horses, but this was over-ruled. The first stone of the new bridge was laid, 'in the presence of a great number of persons of quality and distinction' on Saturday, 29 April, 1758.

Three days before the bridge was opened for traffic, in June 1759, the Dowager Princess of Wales with her eldest son and other members of the Royal Family passed over the bridge from their home at Kew. According to tradition, it was on Kew Bridge in 1760 that Prince George Frederick met the messenger sent to tell him that his grandfather had died, and that he himself had become the new King.

As well as devoting herself to the needs of her growing family, the bereaved Princess had set herself to enlarge and improve the already splendid grounds that surrounded their home. In 1761, at her behest, William Chambers embarked on the construction of the Great Pagoda, which took six months to build. This extraordinary structure is 163 feet high and divided into ten storeys, and Chambers arranged that there should be a decrease of one foot in diameter and height respectively with each successive storey. It must have been a scintillating sight when it was first finished, for its projecting roofs were covered with iron plates varnished with various colours so that they glistened like rainbows. At the corners were eighty crouched dragons, each beast enclosed in thin tinted glass which produced the most dazzling reflections.

The Pagoda is still a great landmark today, though it has been stripped of its more exotic embellishments.

The new King, George III, had inherited Richmond Lodge, the old family home, when his grandfather died. In 1769, the King decided that the Lodge was too small for his rapidly increasing family, and he instructed Chambers (by that time 'Sir William') to draw up plans for a new and very much larger house. The project was frustrated, though, by the members of the Richmond Vestry, who refused to sell to the King the additional ground needed for the extensions. The King, greatly annoyed, decided to move back to Kew and Richmond Lodge quickly became derelict. The King got Sir William Chambers to build an Observatory close to the site of his old home.

With the Court established more or less permanently at Kew—the King and Queen, after the death of the Dowager Princess in 1772, firmly installed in The White House and their children settled in the old Dutch House, just over the road—the place became a fashionable rendezvous. During the summer months, the public were admitted to the royal gardens on one day each week 'for the amusement of all persons genteelly dressed, by His Majesty's express order'. On those days, Kew Green was thronged with carriages and hundreds of pounds were taken at the bridge in tolls. The sightseers loved watching to see whether Their Majesties would appear at one of the windows to speak to their friends and the royal children pottered away happily in their own little gardens just as if they were commoners. 'The whole was a scene of enchantment and delight', recorded one observer. 'Royalty living among their subjects to give pleasure and to do good.' To get away from all this, the Queen had a little cottage, roofed with thatch, built for herself on the southern verge of the gardens, and there she would go to take tea.

In 1776, the Duke and Duchess of Montrose moved into the big house over the river in Twickenham Park. The Duke—William, the second holder of the title—had lost his sight more than a quarter of a century before, was very deaf, and had legs that were so feeble that he was unable to stand up. The Duchess was in little better case, for she was almost completely immobilised by some obscure form of paralysis. In spite of their varied disabilities, this grand old pair of wrecks, sustained largely by their son and heir, the admirable Lord Graham, managed to receive and give generous hospitality to an unending succession of guests, all of whom, of course, had to be of a suitable social standing.

Among the Montroses' most regular visitors—according to his own account, he used to go to Twickenham Park three or four times in every week—was Horace Walpole, the youngest son of the Sir Robert who had been co-Ranger of Richmond Park.

Horace Walpole lived in a 'little cottage' at Strawberry Hill that he had bought from a Mrs. Chenevix, who kept an amazing toy-shop near Charing Cross. Walpole had fallen in love with the cottage, which had once been the home of Colly Cibber, the dramatist, as soon as he saw it. This is how he described it: 'It is a little play-thing-house that I got out of Mrs. Chenevix's shop, and it is the prettiest bauble you ever saw. It is set in enamelled meadows, with filigree hedges . . . Two delightful roads, that you would call dusty, supply me continually with coaches and chaises; barges as solemn as Barons of the Exchequer move under my window; Richmond Hill and Ham walks bound my prospect . . . I have enough land about to keep such a farm as Noah's when he set up in the ark with a pair of each kind, but my cottage is rather cleaner than I believe his was after they had been cooped up together forty days . . .'

Walpole spent the rest of his life adding extra rooms and features to the cottage, most of them contrived in the Gothic manner. By the time he had finished with it, it had battlements, arches, and painted glass, and a long gallery with a fan-vaulted ceiling not unlike the one in King Henry VII's Chapel in Westminster Abbey. His collections, weird mixtures of the valuable and the trivial, gave the interior of the place the atmosphere partly of a museum, partly of an old curiosity shop. (The house, stripped of its contents, which were auctioned in the nineteenth century, is now a Catholic teachers' training college.)

At the time Horace Walpole was living there, Twickenham was a favourite haunt of highwaymen. In a letter he wrote on 7 October, 1781 to the Countess of Ossory, Walpole described the approach of one of these adventurers:

> Lady Browne and I were as usual going to the Duchess of Montrose at seven o'clock. The evening was very dark. In the close lane under her park pale, and within twenty yards of the gate, a black figure on horseback pushed by between the chaise

and the hedge by my side. I suspected it was a highwayman and so I found did Lady Browne, for she was speaking and stopped. To divert her fears, I was just going to say 'Is not that the apothecary going to the Duchess?' when I heard a voice cry 'Stop!' and the figure came back to the chaise. I had the presence of mind, before I let down the glass, to take out my watch, and stuff it within my waistcoat under my arm. He said, 'Your purse and your watches!' I replied 'I have no watch!' 'Then your purse.' I gave it to him, it had nine guineas. It was so dark that I could not see his hand, but felt him take it. He then asked for Lady Browne's purse and said 'Don't be frightened I will not hurt you.' I said 'No, you won't frighten the lady?' He replied, 'No, I give you my word, I will do no hurt.' Lady Browne gave him her purse, and was going to add her watch, but he said 'I am much obliged to you, I wish you good night!' pulled off his hat and rode away.

'Well,' said I, 'Lady Browne you will not be afraid of being robbed another time, for you see there is nothing in it.' 'Oh! but I am,' she said, 'and now I am in terrors, lest he should return, for I have given him a purse with only bad money that I carry on purpose.' 'He certainly will not open it directly', said I 'and at worst he can only wait for us on our return, but I will send my servant back for a horse and a blunderbuss,' which I did.

The next distress was not to terrify the Duchess, who is so paralytic and nervous. I therefore made Lady Browne go into the parlour and desired one of the Duchess' servants to get her a glass of water, while I went into the Drawing Room to break it to the Duchess. 'Well', said I, laughing to her and the rest of the company 'You won't get much from us tonight.' 'Why' said one of them 'have you been robbed?' 'Yes a little,' said I. The Duchess trembled, but it went off. Her Groom of the Chambers said not a word, but slipped out and Lady Margaret and Miss Howe having servants there on horseback he gave them pistols and despatched them different ways. This was exceedingly clever for he knew the Duchess would not have suffered it, as lately, he had detected a man who had robbed her garden and she would not allow him to take up the fellow . . .

The break-up of the royal home at Kew may be said to have started when King George III's mysterious malady became serious, and he was advised (or compelled) by his ignorant doctors to retire to Windsor. He did not often return to Kew after that, and although his sons took houses there—Ernest, Duke of Cumberland, went to live in a house on the north side of the Green, and the Duke of Cambridge in the house with the portico close to the church—by the time Queen Charlotte died in the Dutch House in 1818 the last links between the Royal Family and the little riverside village were ready to be snapped.

The break-up of the great Twickenham Park estate happened at roughly the same time. The dissipation of this ancient piece of land may be said to have started before the Montroses went to live there, when the place was still in the hands of an old Lady Mountrath who was, as Horace Walpole put it, 'as rich and tipsy as Cacafogo in the comedy'. Three days after the old lady breathed her last, Walpole was to write: 'My Lady Mountrath is dead and has made as drunken a Will as you could expect.' The tangles in the drunken will were not to be properly sorted out until 1803, when all its complicated provisions were at last resolved, and the beneficiaries, relieved to be able to come at long last into their own, put the estate on the market. When the estate had remained unsold for a considerable time, the vendors divided their inheritance and offered it for sale in at least two separate lots.

The old house that had been lived in by Bacon and the flat parkland that surrounded it was eventually bought for £16,000 by a London banker named Francis Gosling who already owned a large house in nearby Isleworth. The fabric of the historic old mansion was not in a very good state. (The Duchess of Newcastle, who had lived in it for a few years before it was taken by the Montroses, had said, after she moved out, that she was sorry to leave it, but, indeed, she had inhabited the old place until the boards of the floors had played under her feet 'like the keys of a harpsichord'.) Having a comfortable home of his own downstream, Gosling had most, if not all, of the old mansion pulled down, and he prepared to build on the land.

By 1831, at least eleven private houses had been built and sold on the Twickenham side of the Park. The northern side—the side, that is, nearest Isleworth—had been bought by the Earl of Cassilis (afterwards, the 'First Marquis of Ailsa') and he had rebuilt the house Francis Gosling had owned in Isleworth, re-naming it 'St. Margaret's'. The name, now, is applied to the whole of the district in the immediate vicinity of the Marquis of Ailsa's Twickenham seat. It is one of London's least suburban and most enjoyable suburbs.

Credit for the happy development of St. Margaret's must be given, principally, to the gentlemen who founded the Conservative Land Society in 1852. Twenty years earlier, the Great Reform Act had extended the privilege of voting in parliamentary elections to all those householders who occupied properties worth £50, annual value (in the counties) and £10, annual value (in the boroughs).

'Right', said the people who formed the Conservative Land Society. 'By our enterprise, based on co-operation and mutual assistance, we will develop, for residential purposes, some excellent land in what was once the old Twickenham Park, and by our efforts artisans, members of the professions, officers in the armed services and many others will be able to obtain the most ancient mode of suffrage in this country—the Freehold Franchise.'

In the process of providing a number of worthy men with the chance to vote, the members of the society, under the Chairmanship of Viscount Ranelagh, managed to create one of the finest of all 'garden suburbs'—a well-treed residential area, laid out in an admirable way, with elegantly curved roads and three carefully maintained pleasure grounds. The garden suburbs at Bedford Park, Hampstead, Letchworth and Welwyn, all of which have been highly praised, were not planned until after St. Margaret's was already mature. Moreover, the schedule attached to the original Deed of Covenant (dated August 1854) shows that the members of the society did indeed achieve their aim in attracting a wide spread of trades and professions. Their houses were sold to a banker, a chemist and dentist of George Street, Richmond, a boot and shoe maker, a worsted dealer, a wine merchant, several accountants, a farmer, a general agent, a gardener, an architect, a clerk in a public office, a parliamentary agent, a professor, a cheesemonger, a draper, a brush maker, a schoolmaster; and there are many more.

Cars cross Twickenham Bridge today at the rate of some hundreds per hour. As they drive westwards, the drivers of the vehicles leaving London pass, without seeing it, between Ailsa Road and St. George's Road, one of the most delightful pleasure gardens in all the suburbs of London. The little park, surrounded entirely by beautifully kept private houses, is really a 'water garden', its most unusual feature being a canal, nearly a thousand feet long, that was dug by the monks of 'Syon' some five and a half centuries ago. The iron footbridges, made in an oriental style, that span the lake, and the high alder, plane, cedar and poplar trees that surround it make the garden seem like one of the Chinese landscapes portrayed on so much eighteenth-century English porcelain. Walking in it, one might be walking into the Full Nankin Pattern printed on, say, a Caughley plate or coaching pot.

In 1841, Kew Gardens were handed over to the nation and Sir William Hooker became the first official director. (Though Sir Joseph Banks had been a director, in effect, for forty-seven years.) The gardens were soon developed into one of the most important botanical institutions in the world, with libraries, museums, and living collections which now comprise more than 25,000 different kinds of plant. Among the immense greenhouses that provide protection for the less hardy specimens are the Temperate House, which is about one-eighth of a mile in length, and the lovely Palm House, both made from designs by Decimus Burton. Kew originated the plantation industry of rubber and today still plays an international part in plant introduction and as a quarantine station.

Admission to the Gardens costs, at the time this book is being written, just one penny. In summer, especially on Saturdays and Sundays, the quiet residential roads round the entrances become like crowded car parks, and those parts of the Gardens that lie nearest to the main Kew to Richmond main road are thronged with visitors from every part of the world. But comparatively few people venture to go far from the better-worn paths. In the quieter plantations, like the one in which Queen Charlotte had her thatched cottage built, it is still possible to think some very green thoughts, without being disturbed.

Wherever one looks in the Gardens one can find things to interest and amuse. In 1761, for instance, the Dowager Princess of Wales had a Great Stove built, to keep Kew Palace warm. To grow round one end of it, she had planted a *wisteria sinensis*. This wisteria is still growing sturdily in the open at Kew today, and flowering, though the stove is no longer there. The old climber is supported by an iron frame specially put up for the purpose when the house was demolished in 1861.

The influence of the Gardens can be felt all through the Kew district today, not only because the Pagoda and the giant flagstaff can be seen from most parts of the parish, but because the privately-owned gardens in the vicinity of the Botanical Gardens seem to be rather fuller of unusual plants than gardens are in other suburbs of London, and flowers in them seem to acquire some extra qualities from having such illustrious neighbours. It is a suburb much favoured by artists, writers, publishers and B.B.C. commentators.

The name 'Twickenham' means to most people, now, rugby football matches, for the stadium at which these are held attracts great crowds to what was once tranquil riverside ground. Religious conventions are held in the Twickenham stadium too, outside the football season. And, at the artist Sir Godfrey Kneller's old home, most of the Army's musicians are trained. No one living in Twickenham today can accuse the place of being too quiet.

CHAPTER FIFTEEN

Ham and Petersham: Kingston and Hampton

THE ground on each side of the Thames, upstream from Richmond, has for many centuries been thought a desirable place to live provided one could find a place that would be relatively free from flooding.

When King George II's charming and intelligent mistress Henrietta Howard wanted a summer home, for instance, she chose to build at Marble Hill one of the loveliest houses in the country surrounding London. The design of the superbly simple but well-proportioned villa was based on a sketch made by the architect Colin Campbell, but the influence of Lord Herbert, the future Earl of Pembroke, can be seen all through the house. (The Great Room is clearly modelled on Inigo Jones' famous Double Cube Room at Wilton, which was Lord Herbert's family seat.) The actual building of the house was entrusted to Roger Morris.

When Mrs. Howard retired from Court life in 1734 (by that time she was the Countess of Suffolk) she settled down with the greatest of pleasure to live at Marble Hill: and who would not enjoy living in such a splendid setting? In the house and gardens she entertained Alexander Pope, who lived about a mile upstream and who helped her to lay out the grounds, Dean Swift, John Gay (of 'The Beggar's Opera') and a host of other literary men, musicians and artists, so that her home became almost like another Court, but a more entertaining one than that surrounding the King. After she died in 1767, the house passed through various hands, being rented for a year, in 1795, by Mrs. Fitzherbert, another Royal mistress. The house, which is now a little less glamorously the property of the Greater London Council, has been expertly restored and redecorated and is open to the public.

Over the river from Marble Hill lie Petersham and Ham. The land on the south bank of the Thames between Richmond and

Ham belonged, at the time of the Domesday Survey, to Chertsey Abbey, and the manor was called 'Patrichesam'. When the great catalogue was compiled, the place consisted merely of a church, three acres of meadow, a little arable ground served by fifteen villeins, and a fishery that contained a thousand lampreys. Today cows still graze contentedly in the lush meadows, and the place is noted for the comparatively large number of handsome mansions it contains.

Ham House, the mansion built in 1610 for Sir Thomas Vavasour, passed in the middle of the seventeenth century into the possession of the enormously wealthy Dysart family and was furnished by them, according to John Evelyn, 'like a great Prince's'. (Much of the fine furniture collected by the Dysarts is still there, together with their tapestries and pictures.)

On 17 February, 1672, Elizabeth, Countess of Dysart, was married in Petersham Church. The bride, whose father had been whipping-boy to Charles I, was a widow who had borne eleven children to her previous husband, six of whom had died. She had once been a greaty beauty, but according to one Vicar of Petersham, who acted as a local historian, 'covetousness, ambition and pride had ravaged her comeliness and left their marks on her face'. The bridegroom was John Maitland, Second Duke of Lauderdale. ('A great gorilla of a man, with uncouth body and a shambling gait, a massive head crowned with a disorderly tangle of red hair, and when he spoke he slobbered.') Lauderdale, who, according to some authorities, had been prepared to rescue King Charles I when he was being held at Hampton Court and who, following the younger Prince Charles to Worcester, had certainly been taken prisoner there, had been blatantly carrying on with the Countess of Dysart during her first husband's lifetime. This affair had embittered the Duke's relations with his own wife, and had shocked even the permissive members of Charles II's Court. The pair were joined in Holy Matrimony by the Bishop of Worcester, whom they had taken to the church with them in their carriage.

During the next few years, Ham House was a great centre for jobbery and intrigue. The Duke regularly entertained his fellow members of the notorious 'Cabal' there—the Lords Clifford, Arlington, Buckingham and Ashley—but he, being Scottish, was less responsible to the English parliament than they were, and, besides, he had much more personal influence with the King. The Duchess had been making a lot of money by patronage even while she had been merely the Duke's mistress. Once she was his wife, and so much closer to the Throne, she was able to add trafficking in honours to her other sources of income. At last, on 8 May, 1679, the English parliament presented an Address to the King asking that Lauderdale might be removed from his councils and presence and from all offices of trust. The Duke was clever enough, and well enough liked by the King, to survive.

Among the many other old and admirable houses in the area are Rutland House—built in the year of the Fire of London as a country retreat for Sir William Bolton, who had been a Lord Mayor of the City—and Petersham House, which was built about 1670 for Colonel Thomas Panton, who was then Keeper of Richmond Park. Petersham House, being now National Trust property, is open to the public during specified hours.

After passing through Richmond or Kew, with their mellow Greens nearly surrounded by elegant old houses, and over Ham Common, which is also architecturally delightful, it is always something of a shock to enter Kingston-on-Thames. For Kingston has played just as important a part in English history as the other places have. Unfortunately, Kingston has all too little left to show for its romantic past. Today, it seems a rather ordinary little market town, with one or two quite good stores.

For a thousand years at least, and probably for twice as long as that, Kingston has been a major trading centre, and a place through which Kings, Queens and courtiers have ceaselessly passed and in which, occasionally, they have stayed. The reason for its importance has been largely geographical: this is the first place above London, except Brentford, where the river is quite easy to ford. Some historians believe that it was here that Julius Caesar and his men passed through, or over, the Thames on their way to survey the land Caesar was determined to conquer.

Kingston's only real relic of its remote past is a block of grey sandstone that can now be seen just outside the Guildhall. According to tradition, at least seven Saxon Kings were sitting on this stone—separately, of course—when they were crowned.

The historical value of the stone, or its possible historical value, has only been realised in comparatively recent times. In 1703, the 'square smooth stone in Court Hall' was actually given away by Kingston's civic authorities, who wanted it to be marked with a suitable inscription and set up over 'ye Free Gramer School'. By 1724, the authorities must have got the stone back again, for according to their records they were instructing their Chamberlain in that year to 'forthwith remove the Pebble Stone that now lyes near Doctor Cranmer's doores' and to put it under the Court Hall, 'there to remayne till further orders'. From the Court Hall, the stone was taken to the Saxon Chapel of St. Mary, which was being used at that time as a storehouse for all the municipal junk. When part of the Chapel collapsed, through neglect, the stone was pulled out of the ruins and set up near the old Tudor Guildhall where, the authorities thought, it could be used as a public mounting block. (For mounting horses, that is.)

In the middle of the nineteenth century, one of the town's Aldermen, who was seriously troubled by the disrespect with which the old Coronation Stone was being treated, collected the respectable sum of £450 to pay for its rehabilitation. As a result of the Alderman's efforts, the stone was moved to a prominent site near the Market, set on an impressive plinth, and enclosed by protective railings suitably wrought 'in the Saxon style'. A public holiday was declared, to celebrate this historic occasion, and a special commemorative medal was struck. Thousands of loyal citizens of Kingston gathered to watch their Mayor, a Mr. William Pamphilon, unveil the impressively promoted mounting block, and the Provincial Grand Master of the Freemasons of Surrey, in a subsequent ceremony, anointed the stone with wine and corn oil. The authorities of the British Museum showed their belief in authenticity of Kingston's Kings' Stone by presenting to the town seven unmistakably genuine Saxon coins. Each of these coins had been struck in the reign of a King who had palpably been crowned within the town's boundaries. Who could argue with that?

In the reigns of King Henry VIII and Queen Elizabeth I, England suffered several disastrous outbreaks of the Plague. During one of those epidemics, medical history was made at Kingston when the local authority set up one of the earliest 'isolation hospitals' ever seen in England. The closeness of Kingston to the royal palaces at Hampton Court and Richmond must have made Queen Elizabeth specially conscious of what was going on there, for she was soon urging the Lord Mayor and Aldermen of the City of London to follow the examples of their brothers up the river: 'For we have seen of late an experience in the towne of Kingstone where the infection did begin very hotlie and in restrayninge and keepinge in those that were infected, the same is ceased. They presentlie upon the fyrste infection, caused an house to be made in the fields dystante from the towne, where the infected might be kept apart and provided for all things convenient for their sustenance and care which, yf so little a town as Kingstone is able to performe, we cannott but thinck that the Cittye of London should . . .'

The Kingston justices, at that time, must also have been unusually keen. On 8 September, 1572, the Parish Registers had this entry: 'This day in this towne was kept the Sessions of gayle [gaol] Delyverye and her was hangid six persons and seventene taken for roges and vagabonds and whyppid abowte the market place and brent in the ears . . .'

The town's Chamberlain's accounts for 1681 mention 'thirty-three foot of timber to make the gallows' and a payment of four shillings was made by the authorities in the same year 'to three men for bringing one hundred of Bavins [bundles of brushwood] and fifty fagotts to burne ye woman'. One of the most ferocious purges of all was reported in the *European Magazine* of 1795: 'Very near thirty years ago a remarkable execution happened no further off than Kingston-upon-Thames in Surrey. One Gregory was hanged for horse stealing, and at the same time no less than eleven of his own sons were hung by his side on the same gallows for repeated crimes of the same nature; and, what is yet more singular, one Colman, with his five sons, were hung on the same gallows at the same moment, in all eighteen in number . . .'

Kingston was a particularly unhealthy place in which to live, during the nineteenth century. Serious epidemics were frequent in the district, and the death rate exceptionally high. This is hardly surprising, when the little working-class cottages of the town could earn, in October 1860, this gruesome description in the pages of the *Surrey Comet*: 'They possess no outlet whatever at the back, not even a window, so that the air cannot pass freely through them and the ceiling of the rooms are so low that a man of ordinary height cannot stand upright in them. They are destitute of the most common necessaries for decency, one water closet being made to serve several dwellings. Some are without a sink of any kind, and the dirty water is brought out and emptied into the uneven gutters in the centre of the lane, and may be seen standing in fetid pools.'

The disposal of the town's sewage was a constant source of anxiety to the local authority at that time. In May 1865, the construction of a new and ambitious underground drainage system was started. It was completed just twelve months later, and cost the town the very considerable sum of sixteen thousand pounds. Unfortunately for the rate-payers, the new drains had two serious disadvantages. They were shoddily built, so that within a very short time the brickwork was a mass of leaks and, those parts of their contents that did not actually escape on the journey flowed eventually, in accordance with the custom of the times, into the Thames. Before the drains had been in use for two years, an Act of Parliament was passed that compelled all local authorities upstream from London to divert their sewage from the Thames so that part at least of the drinking water needed for the capital could be drawn from the river. Fines of £100 per day could be imposed on any authority that was unable, or unwilling, to comply.

After a lot of hard talking, the Kingston councillors managed to obtain a temporary reprieve from the full severities of this Act. But the town's wise men knew that they would eventually have to find an answer to their drainage problem. After several misguided ventures, they hit on a wholly satisfactory solution: they came to an arrangement with a firm called the 'Native Guano Company'. Under this arrangement the company agreed to set up a sophisticated chemical processing plant in the Down Hall Meadow, which is a little to the north of Kingston's railway bridge. On this site, the company undertook to separate the town's outflow into effluence that could be safely discharged into the Thames, and sludge which could be dried, ground, and sold at the modest price of three shillings per hundredweight to horticulturists. Soon, 'Kingston Native Guano' was being used in all parts of Britain. In a leaflet widely distributed by the Corporation's Fertiliser Department, the advantages of the Guano were brought to the notice of all keen gardeners who had not heard of it. So that no one should fail to guess the origin and purpose of the substance on offer, the scribe who compiled the leaflet included, tactfully, a quotation from Shakespeare's *Timon of Athens*: 'The Earth's a thief that feeds and breeds by a composture stolen from general excrement . . .'

Until the Second World War, Kingston had managed to retain a little of its leisurely medieval atmosphere, but since then, in spite of some occasional Morris dancing on the lawn in front of the parish church and the building of an entirely new public house to be called 'The Saxon Kings', the place has become, in the words of one of the town's officials, 'just another busy shopping centre'. When, in 1971, the members of the Corporation of Kingston proposed to pull down Picton House, a fine Georgian dwelling that had unfortunately been built on the valuably-sited river bank, there was a public outcry. An Inspector appointed by the Ministry of the Environment to investigate the matter travelled down from Whitehall and found, to his dismay, that Kingston had at that time fewer historic buildings left standing than any other London borough south of the Thames. (There are twenty-eight listed items only. Five of these were churches, four were 'conduit houses' or elaborate drain covers, two were bridges, and two were just blocks of stone.) In the whole of the Greater London area, there were only three boroughs that had cared as little about their heritage from the past—Barking, Brent and Newham—and none of these had had anything like the treasures of Kingston.

It is just possible, though, that sentiment and aesthetic pleasure have given way, in Kingston, to modernity and convenience because there has been for centuries, only a little way up the road, the vast old palace of Hampton Court, which is stuffed full of memories—and ghosts.

The palace was large enough when Cardinal Wolsey owned it, and when the poet John Skelton could write:

> Why come ye not to Court?
> To whyche court?
> To the Kynges Courte?
> Or to Hampton Court?
> Nay, to the Kynges Courte,
> But Hampton Court
> Hath the preeminence

Even in those early days, there were more than two hundred rooms kept always ready for the entertainment of guests. When King Henry VIII took it over from Wolsey, he added a Great Hall with a magnificent hammerbeam roof, a new court where Wren's Fountain Court now stands, and new blocks on the west front.

Kings Charles I and Charles II both lived happily in the old palace without doing much to increase its size, but from 1689 onwards King William III and Mary his wife kept Sir Christopher Wren busy for several years rebuilding and extending the place so that it should not be outshone by the great Versailles palace of William's principal rival the French King Louis XIV. By the time King William died, in 1702, after being thrown from his horse when it stumbled on a mole hill in the park, Hampton Court had become one of the most admired complexes of buildings in Europe.

So much has happened, in Hampton Court Palace, that it would take a whole book to tell the story. The place has seen the courtship of Ann Boleyn, the birth of the future King Edward VI, the death of Queen Jane Seymour, almost immediately afterwards, the arrest of Queen Catherine Howard for her alleged infidelities, the imprisonment and escape of King Charles I and countless other incidents usually poignant, too often tragic. If people who live in the district do not want to join the fee-paying visitors who pass through the place in throngs, they can always go there at less popular hours to enjoy the beautifully laid out grounds. Among many other delights are a King's Tiltyard planted out with roses, a Broad Walk nearly half a mile long flanked on one side by two of the most splendidly planted and kept up herbaceous borders to be seen in the whole of England, great avenues of trees, a mile-long ornamental canal, a twentieth-century reproduction of a Tudor knot garden, a Great Vine and a famous maze.

Beyond the palace lies Hampton itself, a straggling village, which has round its Green many charming small houses built in the reigns of William and Mary and Queen Anne to accommodate people connected with the Court; half a mile or so upstream is another small cluster of delightful old houses that are grouped round the parish church. David Garrick, the famous actor, lived here once in the most resplendent style. His villa, done up for him by the brothers Adam, is now divided into flats, and modern neo-Georgian houses have been neatly arranged in his garden. *Sic transit Gloria Mundi.*

CHAPTER SIXTEEN

Chiswick, Brentford and Ealing

HAMMERSMITH is being pulled down and rebuilt so rapidly, as this book is being written, that it is really not safe to say much about it, other than that it contains a very beautiful piece of civil engineering—the Flyover—that may be judged by posterity to be one of the better works of art of the present century.

On the north bank of the Thames, as one moves away from Hammersmith, one comes to Chiswick. Not very long ago, Chiswick was a quiet, nightingale-haunted village surrounded by fields and market gardens. Today, it is a crowded suburb divided inexorably into two parts by the ever-roaring 'Cromwell Road Extension' that comes down off the aforesaid Flyover. Life in the land immediately to the north and south of this monstrous highway is dominated by noise and the ceaseless rush of traffic. There are three relatively quiet corners in Chiswick, however, that are sufficient compensation for the horrors of the Great West Road. They are Chiswick Mall, the extensive grounds that surround Chiswick House, and Strand-on-the-Green.

Chiswick Mall has the same kind of slightly dotty charm as many of the small seaport towns that were built principally in the eighteenth and early nineteenth centuries. The period houses, which look down directly on to the Thames, are different, in nearly every instance, from their immediate neighbours, which produces a pleasing variety. Many of the houses have balconies, conservatories, ox-eye windows, or other agreeable features. Some have small private gardens on the river side of the approach road. (Very useful for party-giving on the day of the Universities' Boat Race.) It is a peaceful backwater that has traditionally attracted writers, artists and actors. Sir Alan Herbert ('A. P. Herbert') had his home for many years at the Hammersmith end of The Mall and from time to time there have been Redgraves hereabouts. The pub called the 'Lamb Tap' in Church Street, which leads off The Mall, has been used, through long periods of history, for inquests on people found drowned in the vicinity. That is the kind of inconsequential place it has been.

Chiswick House—'Too little to live in, and too big to hang on a watch chain'—is a landmark in the history of English buildings and a monument to eighteenth-century elegance. It is beautifully kept up today, and open to the public.

The original Chiswick House was an early seventeenth-century 'Jacobean' mansion. In 1628, it was bought by the First Earl of Burlington. In course of time, the Earl's grandson, Richard Boyle, succeeded to the estate while he was still a child. As a young man, the Third Earl went on the Grand Tour, as it was customary for wealthy young gentlemen to do in those days, and he returned to England filled with enthusiasm for Italy, for the classical architecture he had seen there, and for a young painter, sculptor and architect, William Kent, whom he had found studying in Rome and whom he had brought back with him to this country as a kind of domesticated arbiter of good taste.

The idea of building an entirely new house in the grounds of his Chiswick home was the direct result of Lord Burlington's visits to the Villa Capra, built by Palladio near Vicenza. The work was undertaken more as an architectural study, to provide a supremely refined and decorated pavilion, rather than to provide another residence for the Earl. In its original form, the building comprised a set of ornate state or reception rooms grouped round an octagonal central hall. (The names of these rooms—the Red Velvet Room, which has a painted ceiling designed by William Kent, the Blue Velvet Room, the Green Velvet Room, the Red Closet and the Gallery—only partly suggest their opulence and the variety of their enrichments.) The rooms in the lower storey were occupied by Lord Burlington's library.

The gardens at Chiswick took twenty years to lay out, being reasonably complete by 1736. 'I can assure you Chiswick has been to me the finest thing this glorious sun has shined upon', Alexander Pope wrote to Lord Burlington, four years before that. In front of the centre of the Villa Burlington and Kent made a great avenue of cedar and lime trees, four hundred feet long, which ended in a circular 'exedra' (a place for sitting, and conversation) made from clipped myrtle, in the niches of which were placed valuable vases and antique statues. Three of these, representing Caesar, Pompey and Cicero, had been brought from the Emperor Hadrian's Villa at Tivoli. Most of the elegant garden buildings designed by Burlington and Kent, including the Cassina, the Pavilion by the lake, and the Orangery, have now disappeared, but the serpentine canal itself, spanned by a Classic Bridge designed by Benjamin Wyatt, is still one of the most attractive features of the grounds. The lake used to terminate in an architectural Cascade, the water for which was raised by a 'Hydraulic Machine' based on an Archimedean Screw, but this too, alas, has disappeared.

In 1749, William Hogarth, the distinguished but then largely unappreciated painter and engraver, took a summer villa with a large garden at Chiswick. Hogarth's 'little country box', which used to stand in a quiet lane that led from Duke's Avenue to Chiswick church, can still be seen and visited, but now it is right by the resounding Great West Road and dwarfed by the factories (Reckitt and Colman, and Cherry Blossom Boot Polish) and the laundry (The 'Hogarth') that hem it in. The filbert avenue in which the great artist used to play ninepins and his workshop have entirely disappeared.

Hogarth detested William Kent, who had been installed so comfortably for so long in Lord Burlington's town house, saying of him that 'Neither England nor Italy produced a more contemptible dauber than Kent'. He caricatured without mercy the altar-piece that Kent had painted for the church of St. Clement Dane's in the Strand, burlesquing the feeble composition and weak draughtsmanship which finally persuaded Bishop Gibson to have the painting removed from the church. Kent had sufficient influence at Court to be able to retaliate by squashing a proposal that Hogarth should be invited to paint portraits of the Royal Family. Lacking many important commissions, then, Hogarth spent much of his time at Chiswick doing research into the mysterious serpentine 'Line of Beauty and of Truth' which, he contended, was the underlying principle of enjoyment of beauty in life, as well as in art. The great artist was buried, when he died in 1764, just outside Chiswick church, on the river side. David Garrick put up the tomb, with its urn, and composed the epitaph:

> Farewell, great painter of mankind,
> Who reached the noblest point of art,
> Whose pictured morals charm the mind
> And through the eye correct the heart.

If Genius fire thee, Reader, stay;
If Nature touch thee, drop a tear;
If neither move thee, turn away,
For Hogarth's honoured dust lies here.

Close to Hogarth's tomb lies James Whistler (1834–1903), who admired Hogarth's work so much that he wanted to be buried near him. Near him, too, by one of life's crueller ironies, lies the hated William Kent.

When Lord Burlington, of Chiswick House, died in 1753, he left an only daughter who married the fourth Duke of Devonshire. Their son had the original Jacobean mansion pulled down in 1788, and as the little Palladian villa was not large enough to accommodate an aristocratic family with all the servants an aristocratic family of that time needed, he had wings built on to the original structure. (They have recently been removed, so that the Villa stands today as nearly as possible as its creators intended.)

Georgiana, Duchess of Devonshire, entertained lavishly in the Villa, and her friend Charles James Fox died in one of its rooms. (So, too, later, did Edward Canning.) The subsequent Dukes and Duchesses of Devonshire were equally hospitable. On 17 May, 1828, Sir Walter Scott wrote in his *Diary*: 'Drove to Chiswick, where a numerous and gay party were enabled to walk and enjoy the beauties of that Palladian dome. The place and ornamental gardens belonging to it resemble a picture of Watteau. The scene was dignified by the presence of an immense elephant who, under the charge of a groom, wandered up and down, giving an air of Asiatic pageantry to the entertainment.'

The Villa at Chiswick probably reached the zenith of its glory on Saturday, 8 June, 1844, when the current Duke of Devonshire was honoured by a visit from the Emperor of Russia, the King of Saxony, His Royal Highness Prince Albert and other royal figures, about seven hundred members of the principal noble families of the kingdom also being invited to be present. It was one of the most splendid fêtes ever held in Britain. 'The royal visitors were conducted by their noble host to the Saloon, where the Emperor held a sort of drawing room, at which most of the company were able to be present', wrote Thomas Faulkner, describing the great occasion, in the following year. 'After a sumptuous repast, the royal party retired to the lawn at the back of the villa. About half an hour later, the party moved to the magnificent cedar walk, where, beneath one of the splendid trees, a sort of court was held by the Emperor, surrounded by those only inferior to himself in rank, by whom the rest of the company, from the highest to the most humble, were successively presented to His Majesty. There was an easy freedom in the Emperor's manner which had the effect of entirely removing any degree of restraint that might otherwise have been felt by many persons.'

The very best Regimental Bands played in the grounds on that memorable afternoon. An 'unusual diversion' was caused by the presence of some giraffes which, coming from the Surrey Zoological Garden and being about to be sent to St. Petersburg, were brought down to the Gardens and located on the opposite bank of the serpentine lake. One of the giraffes, to the delight of the guests, waded across the lake in order to be fed by them.

The Chiswick Villa continued to bolster up the Devonshires' own personal image for a few more years. Then, it was leased by them to Edward, Prince of Wales, as a place conveniently close to London in which his family could spend the greater part of their summers. The Marquis of Bute took it after that, and occupied it from 1879 to 1892. In that year, however, all the best furniture and the great works of art were removed by the Devonshires from the house, and it became a private hospital for the wealthy insane. Then, in 1929, having become more than a little decrepit, the Villa was acquired from the Ninth Duke of Devonshire by the Middlesex County Council, the cost being largely defrayed by contributions from King George V, the former Urban District Council of Brentford and Chiswick, and others. It is now looked after by the Ministry of Works, who have cleared out all the woodworm and dry rot, and Burlington and Kent's Great Avenue, flanked by stone urns and sphinx-like figures and shaded by vast cedar trees, has found a new and serious purpose as a splendid children's romping ground—easily one of the grandest in the suburbs of London.

The third relatively quiet corner of Chiswick is Strand-on-the-Green, near Kew Bridge. It is very like Chiswick Mall in character, but seems even quieter, except when there are aircraft roaring overhead, as there is only a pathway, along which motor cars cannot pass, between the houses and the river.

Until the late eighteenth century, there were only a few fishermen's cottages on the river bank at this point. Then, it became quite a fashionable place to live, and some more substantial houses were put up, though none of them were nearly as grand as the best of the houses in Chiswick Mall. In 1780, at one of these houses—it has a terracotta lion over the door—the artist John Zoffany decided to live.

Zoffany was born in 1733 at Ratisbon in Germany. After receiving a training in Rome, he migrated, in 1758, to England. At first, he found it impossible to make a living and is said to have practically starved in a garret in Drury Lane. Then, his plight was made known to Stephen Rimbault, a clock maker of Seven Dials, who employed him to paint decorations on his clocks.

Next, Zoffany became 'drapery painter' and general assistant to Benjamin Wilson, the fashionable portrait painter, who had a studio in Great Queen Street. Some unkind people hinted at the time that Zoffany did, in fact, paint more than just the draperies for his prosperous master. Whether that is true or not he did attract the attention of David Garrick, who was being painted by Wilson in his favourite rôles of 'Hamlet' and 'Romeo', and Garrick invited the young man to his Villa at Hampton.

Wilson, by that time, was openly envious of his assistant's talents and was on the watch for anyone who might want to lure him away. So, he sent Garrick a pseudonymous letter, purporting to have been written by one 'Timothy Lovetruth', in which he complained that Garrick was trying to tempt Zoffany from his properly recompensed duties. Garrick promptly wrote back to 'Timothy Lovetruth', telling him that if his friend Mr. Wilson sent any more spies to report on Zoffany's visits to his country home at Hampton, he, Mr. Garrick, would have them thrown into the river.

Three years after he moved into the house at Strand-on-the-Green with his family, Zoffany decided to leave them there, and to go off to India. (Whether his decision was made from restlessness, or from cupidity, does not seem to be known.) In India, the artist spent six years at the court of the Nabob of Oude, amassing while he was there a very large personal fortune. He returned to his wife and children in 1790 and remained at Strand-on-the-Green for the rest of his life. In St. Paul's Church, at nearby Old Brentford, there is an altar-piece that Zoffany gave to the congregation of the older St. George's Brentford, but which was moved over when that church ceased to be used for services. The painting represents the Last Supper, and contains, in the figure of 'St. Peter', a portrait of Zoffany himself. Fishermen from Brentford and Isleworth are believed to have acted as models for the remaining apostles, and the Zoffanys' negro servant is shown in the foreground. Zoffany is buried in the churchyard at Kew.

Brentford, at the time when Zoffany was living in the neighbourhood, was still known as 'Dirty Brentford'. The poet Thomas Gray said of it: 'Brentford, tedious town, For dirty streets and white-legged chickens known . . .' But it is said to have been much liked by King George I, who found that the genial squalor of its humble dwellings reminded him of his native Hanover. In the frequent journeys he made to and from Hampton Court, the King always chose to be taken along the filthy road that led from Hyde Park Corner through Brentford and Hounslow, rather than by any other better kept up route. The district, today, is in much the same state of reorganisation as Hammersmith, and a lot of its early nineteenth-century industrial architecture is, perhaps necessarily, being tactfully swept away.

Just to the north of Chiswick is a really suburban suburb, which Brentford, even in its prime, never was. The suburb of Bedford Park was started in 1875 in one of the very earliest attempts to create a 'garden environment' for a new residential development. Most of the streets in the new park were given names that had some association with the more genteel sides of eighteenth-century life, and the moderately large houses that they served were designed in a homely, distinctive and partly traditional style. The nucleus of the novel arrangement was a church created by Norman Shaw in a courageous attempt to get away from the neo-Gothic manner that was practically obligatory, for churches, at the time.

The ancient Manor of Gunnersbury, on the fringes of which Bedford Park was set out, is part of the parish of Ealing. The Manor at Gunnersbury has been held, in its time, by some quite notable people. In 1378, for instance, it was the home of Alice Perrers, who was a 'domestic' in the service of Queen Philippa, wife of King Edward III and who, after the Queen's death, became the official mistress of the King. In the eighteenth century, as we have seen, it was taken over by the Princess Amelia when she swept out crossly from The White Lodge in Richmond Park.

More recently, a rebuilt Gunnersbury has been used by members of the very wealthy Rothschild family, and has been one of their more opulently appointed seats. Today, the former Rothschild home is publicly owned, and houses a fine local history museum.

Ealing, where some of the very best British films that have ever been made were produced, during the years that immediately followed the Second World War, was once the scene of a real-life confrontation as dramatic as any that have been put, within its boundaries, on film.

In the year 1776, the Manor House at Ealing was taken by a well-known scholar named Doctor Dodd, who intended to use it as a boarding school for boys. Doctor Dodd was one of the most eloquent and admired preachers of the day; he was the author of several sermons that he had had published, and had promptly become best-sellers; and he was a Chaplain to the King.

Unfortunately for Doctor Dodd, though, he was also a very proud man, and, as the proverb reminds us, pride regrettably tends to come before a fall. Made vain by all the praise that was being showered on him (the kind that is lavished on football strikers and popular singers today) Doctor Dodd started to spend money more freely, despite a handsome income, than money was coming in. Temporarily inconvenienced, as they say, he put his hand quietly and unofficially into a convenient till, knowing, as oh so many persons in positions of trust have known, that he would be able to pay back the sum he had borrowed before anyone had even known it had gone.

Unfortunately for Doctor Dodd, again, he did not get away with it. Mr. Manley, the man who discovered that a bit of financial legerdemain had been going on, told the Criminal Court at the Old Bailey, later, how a bond had come into his hand signed, apparently, by the famous Lord Chesterfield, who was a fellow-Trustee of some charity with the Reverend Accused. Having established the fact that the famous Lord Chesterfield had not, indeed, signed the bond, Mr. Manley had gone to Doctor Dodd's house and had suggested that he, the Reverend Doctor, might have forged the famous Lord Chesterfield's signature. The Reverend Doctor had seemed much distressed by this charge, as well he might, and as soon as he had managed to recover himself, he had explained that only the most urgent necessity had driven him to such a desperate expedient.

No witnesses having been produced who would be daring enough to speak in favour of the prisoner, Doctor Dodd was put into the box to speak in his own defence. He started by saying that he was fully sensible of the heinousness of the crime of forgery, but he called on God to witness that he had meant no injury to anyone. He should have been able to reinstate the money in a few months, he swore it, if only he had been left alone. It was a most cruel prosecution, he went on, since Mr. Manley had suggested that if he, the speaker, made proper restitution, no further action would be taken. Proper restitution had been made, he said, and if he were made to suffer for his indiscretion his dear wife, with whom he had lived for seven and twenty years in the most perfect conjugal happiness and fidelity, and his creditors would suffer as greatly.

In spite of Doctor Dodd's impassioned appeal, the members of the jury brought in a verdict of Guilty. Afterwards, though, these good men and true drew up a Memorial to His Majesty the King recommending that the Reverend Doctor should receive the Royal Mercy, and they presented it in court. A petition also asking for mercy for the Doctor was later presented to His Majesty by the Sheriffs, attended by the Remembrancer, on behalf of the City of London. Another petition was presented, after that, by Lord Percy, signed by 'upwards of twenty thousand of the inhabitants of Westminster'. The pleas of all these worthy people were ignored. Justice, said the King and his immediate advisers, had to take its course.

So, on 27 June, 1776, the wretched Royal Chaplain was taken from Newgate Prison to the gallows at Tyburn in a mourning cart. This is how one eye-witness described the scene:

> The doctor, to all appearances, was rendered perfectly stupid from despair, His hat was flapped all round, and pulled over his eyes, which were never directed to any object around, nor even raised, except now and then lifted up in the course of his prayers. He came in a coach, and a very heavy shower of rain fell just upon entering the cart, and another just upon putting on his nightcap. During the showers an umbrella was held over his head, which Gilly Williams, who was present, observed was quite unnecessary, as the doctor was going to a place where he might be dried. The wind, which was high, blew off his hat,

which rather embarrassed him. There were two clergymen attending him, one of whom seemed much distressed. The executioner took both the hat and the wig off at the same time, why he put on his wig again I do not know, but he did; and the doctor took off his wig a second time, and then tied on a nightcap which did not fit him. I stayed until he was cut down, and put into the hearse.

Ealing, today, retains quite a lot of the semi-countrified charm it had when the ill-fated Doctor Dodd was taken away from the Manor House by the Green. There are several expanses of open ground, one of them—Walpole Park—having been created at the beginning of this century from the grounds of the large mansion, Pitshanger Manor, that now serves as a public library. From 1844 onwards, Pitshanger Manor was the home of the unmarried daughters of the Prime Minister who had been assassinated in the Houses of Parliament in 1812: the Misses Jane, Frances, Maria, Louisa and Frederika Perceval. The last of these tough old spinsters to die was Miss Frederika. She survived until 12 May, 1900.

Another exceptionally tough resident of Ealing was Jean François Gravelet, better known by his pseudonym 'Charles Blondin'. Blondin crossed Niagara Falls on a tightrope 1,100 feet long and 160 feet above the water in 1859. He repeated this feat several times, and always with some daring innovation. He did it blindfolded, in a sack, pushing a wheelbarrow, on stilts and carrying a man on his back. Once, he even sat down half-way across and made and ate an omelette. His connection with Ealing is commemorated by the names of two streets, Blondin and Niagara Avenues.

Between Ealing and Harrow, where this circuitous survey of London's suburbs started, lie Perivale, Greenford and Wood End. The first of these, just off the busy Western Avenue, is rather dominated by the Hoover Company's factory and other industrial buildings. Greenford, too, has lost most of its 'village' atmosphere during the present century and is no longer one of London's most charming suburbs. By the time one reaches Wood End, the skyline is given some romantic interest, once again, by the slopes of The Hill at Harrow. But that is where our journey started, and there must end.

EPILOGUE

In the jaunty and optimistic days of the Prince Regent, people living in his capital city could be heard singing:

London is the place for me,
There everything is moving,
There things are changing every day,
And everything's improving

One could well ask how many dwellers in the suburbs of London would join in that chorus today? Even while this book was being written, great changes have been made in the places with which it deals, and only a born liar or a plausible public relations officer could keep up any pretence that the alterations make Greater London a pleasanter place in which to live.

Prime among all the blights that have been spreading over the suburbs of London in the past few years has been the awful blight of monotony. As we have seen, the disease got an ineradicable foothold in some of the suburbs that were rushed up quickly for profit in the great housing booms of the late Victorian and Edwardian eras, and in the years between the two World Wars. These dreary places were greatly outnumbered, though, by the older suburbs that contained apparently inexhaustible pockets of interest.

This state of affairs continued until the late 1960s and early 1970s, when 'development' became a fashionable word, and rich speculators moved massively into many of the Metropolitan Area's most charming and best-loved districts. Then, late Georgian and early Victorian villas and small terraces were knocked down like ninepins, to be replaced by buildings of a depressing uniformity. Small family-owned shops in which it was a pleasure to browse disappeared for ever and, in their place, came vast supermarkets in which the wares are packed and displayed with skill, but also with deadening regularity. (A supermarket and its surroundings in Ealing or Hounslow may well look exactly like a supermarket and its surroundings in Hendon or Enfield, and each will probably be indistinguishable from the other.) So, the individual character of many of London's suburban shopping streets has been recently effaced, and all these thoroughfares tend, now, to look approximately identical.

With the increase in general prosperity suggested by Mr. Harold Macmillan's famous 'never had it so good' slogan, there has come, too, a corresponding increase in the amount of traffic passing along London's suburban roads. The so-called 'South Circular Road', for instance, that passes through Putney and East Sheen is not very much wider than it was when horse-drawn coaches rolled in leisurely fashion along it, stopping perhaps at the Hare and Hounds or at the Bull. Today, the Upper Richmond Road at Sheen has to accommodate an almost endless stream of tinny vehicles which pass along it in an aggressive nose-to-rear-bumper fashion. Crossing the road has become for pedestrians a stimulating and highly hazardous adventure, and the raised 'islands' in the middle of the road have become refuges on which the fearful, the slow-witted and the disabled are liable to be marooned for long periods of time. On this and similar suburban roads the strident alarms emitted by ambulances are now familiar sounds.

As pollution on the roads has rapidly made life in some suburbs of London—Blackheath and Clapham, for example—almost intolerable in recent years, so, too, pollution from the air has made life in many other suburbs equally unpleasant. Relentlessly, now, jumbo jets and comparable monsters stream down over the suburbs of West London on their way to the airport at Heathrow. The insufferable noise these great aircraft make drowns the sweet sound of birdsong in Richmond Park and the Botanical Gardens at Kew. And, the roaring beasts leave behind them in their slip-streams long black trails of greasy smoke. Inexorably, the impurities drift earthwards and into the homes—and lungs—of the dwellers in the suburbs principally affected. It would not be at all surprising if some one, some day, who wants to strike a historic blow for the liberty of the subject sets up a real live anti-aircraft gun in his trim little back garden in the suburbs of London, and in a moment of monumental exasperation presses the trigger. One of the most effective individual protests of all time will have been made and the 'special measures' which, it is rumoured, the authorities have ready for just such an emergency will be given a full-scale test.

Noisy, dirty, and motor-car-ridden though London's suburbs may have become, they still provide 'Ideal Homes' for hundreds of thousands of people who would never live anywhere else, even if they had the opportunity. The Wolf Cubs who have just joined the Second Mortlake Scout Troop skip happily beside their parents after school on Tuesday evenings to the corrugated iron hut by Watney's Brewery as Mortlake's little boys have done, to the author's knowledge, for the past forty years or more. (The Cubs of this generation may have longer hair, under their green and gold caps, than their predecessors, but in no other respect do they seem any different.) The suburban cinemas still attract loyal crowds of regular patrons, though now these buildings are more likely to be used for Bingo than for films. And there are signs of hope for the future in the rapid growth of interest in the local Amenities Societies and other associations of public-spirited people who want to see the environment improve and the quality of suburban life get better and better. The great 'Live in Metroland' dream may have been an illusion, but it is not going to be allowed to turn into a nightmare.

SUGGESTIONS FOR FURTHER READING

J. Harvey Bloom, M.A.: *Bygone Balham and Tooting Bec*. London: Mitchell, Hughes and Clarke 1926.

Guy Boas, C. S. Cloake and H. J. Warren: *Wimbledon—Has a History*. Wimbledon: The John Evelyn Society 1967.

J. H. Michael Burgess: *The Chronicles of Clapham*. Privately printed 1929.

Cecil T. Davis: *Wandsworth Historical Jottings*. Geo. Cable, Wandsworth 1905.

Warwick Draper: *Chiswick*. London: Anne Bingley 1973.

Leland L. Duncan, M.V.O., F.S.A.: *History of the Borough of Lewisham*. Charles North, the Blackheath Press 1908.

The Diary of John Evelyn.

Alan Glencross: *The Buildings of Greenwich*. London Borough of Greenwich.

G. W. C. Green, B.A.: *The Story of Wandsworth and Putney*. London: Sampson Low, Marston and Co. Ltd.

Nigel Hamilton: *Guide to Greenwich*. The Greenwich Bookshop.

Ernest Hammond: *Bygone Putney*. Kingston-on-Thames: The Surrey Comet 1898.

Pamela Fletcher Jones: *Richmond Park, Portrait of a Royal Playground*, Phillimore and Co., London and Chichester 1972.

Dorothy McCall: *When That I Was*. London: Faber and Faber 1952.

William Myson, F.L.A., and J. G. Berry, N.D.H., F. Inst. P.R.A.: *Cannizaro House, Wimbledon, and its Park*. Wimbledon: The John Evelyn Society 1972.

The Diary of Samuel Pepys.

Joanna Richardson: *The Disastrous Marriage*. London: Jonathan Cape 1960.

Michael Robbins: *New Survey of England: Middlesex*. London: Collins and Company 1953.

Lloyd Sanders: *Old Kew, Chiswick and Kensington.* London: Methuen and Company 1910.

Aileen Smiles: *Samuel Smiles and His Surroundings.* London: Robert Hale 1956.

Fred Turner: *History and Antiquities of Brentford.* Walter Pearce and Company 1922.

Alan C. B. Urwin: *Twicknam Parke.* Printed by Thomasons Limited, Hounslow 1965.

INDEX